Ernest Geldart, Edward Young Cox

The Art of Garnishing Churches at Christmas and Other

Times

A manual of directions

Ernest Geldart, Edward Young Cox

The Art of Garnishing Churches at Christmas and Other Times
A manual of directions

ISBN/EAN: 9783337411633

Printed in Europe, USA, Canada, Australia, Japan

Cover: Foto ©Lupo / pixelio.de

More available books at **www.hansebooks.com**

THE ART

OF

Garnishing ✝ Churches

AT

CHRISTMAS AND OTHER TIMES.

A Manual of Directions.

EDITED AND RE-WRITTEN

BY

THE REV. ERNEST GELDART,

Rector of Little Braxted, Essex.

With Plates by the Editor, and an Appendix,

CONTAINING A CATALOGUE OF MATERIALS, &c., &c.

———✦———

SOLD BY

COX SONS, BUCKLEY & Co., 29, SOUTHAMPTON STREET,
LONDON.

1882.

LONDON:

ROBERTS & LEETE, 57 & 58, TOOLEY STREET, SOUTHWARK, S.E.,

AND 6, LIME STREET SQUARE, E.C.

CORRIGENDA.

Page 16, line 25, *add* (Fig. 2, Pl. III.)

  ,, 17 ,, 18, *for* crochets, *read* crockets.

  ,, 20 ,, 2, *for* or, *read* of.

  ,, 34 (bottom), *for* quartrefoils, *read* quatrefoils.

  ,, 37, line 7, *for* Pls., *read* Pss.

  ,, 43 ,, 4 (right column), *omit* procedentem a.

  ,, 47 ,, 7, *for* meœ, filis, *read* meae, filiis.

  ,, 52 ,, 12, *for* pontes, *read* frontes.

  ,, 52 ,, 13, *for* antem, *read* autem.

  ,, 52 ,, 31, *for (d), read (e); for* floreated, *read* floriated.

  ,, 57, *add*—S. Nicomede. A club set with spikes.

  ,, 57 ,, S. Swithun. A shower of rain.

  ,, 65, (note), *for* sarum colouris, *read* Sarum colours.

  ,, 68, line 12, *for* sketch, *read* stretch.

There are many minor misprints and errors of punctuation, for which indulgence is asked until a new edition is called for.

E. G.

PREFACE TO THE FIRST EDITION.

THE following pages are intended to serve as a plain practical compendium of the Art of Garnishing Churches at Christmas and other Festivals. The principles of the art are briefly discussed, and the rules for applying them are given so fully that they will, it is hoped, suffice for the guidance of the most inexperienced amateurs.

The subject has been considered solely in its æsthetical aspects. A great diversity of opinion prevails as to the proper limits of Ecclesiastical Decoration; but the Author has entirely abstained from entering into that controversy. He has contented himself with giving designs and methods, varying widely in character, and suitable, some to the most elaborately, and some to the most simply decorated edifices.

Every available treatise relating to the present and allied subjects has been considered. The information derived from these sources has been combined with the results of the Author's own practical experience—which is considerable—and with the valuable suggestions of several clergymen and others, who have successfully practised the beautiful art, which applies some of Nature's gifts to illustrate the successive seasons of the Christian year.

A grateful acknowledgment is due to several friends for the useful information contributed by them, and particularly to Mr. S. J. Nicholl and Mr. B. J. Talbert, for several designs which illustrate these pages.

EDWARD YOUNG COX.

October, 1868.

CONTENTS.

— —✦— —

PREFACE.

APPENDIX.

Containing Price List and Descriptive Catalogue of Materials used in Church Decoration.

PREFACE TO THE PRESENT BOOK.

KINDLY READER,

One of the *first* difficulties in writing this book, though (as is customary) the *last* encountered, was the character which I should assume to you in the Preface; whether Editor, Author or Corrector.

The publishers put into my hands some months ago the last edition ot the "Art of Garnishing," and requested me to "*re*-write" it, suggesting that my pencil as well as my pen should be used within the like wide range.

In sending these sheets and plates to the printer with a view to their meeting your eyes, my reader, I send as the result of my labours, the "re-writing" and the "re-drawing" of nearly every page. Still how far my work is *original* (the writing at least) I scarcely know, for paste and scissors have been freely employed.

Differences of style may here and there betray the patches on the garment, but as I have neither desire to take the praise of others nor to bear the blame, it may be well to state as far as possible what is new and what old.

The historical notes are from the former book; the list of texts in great measure, the directions for making wreaths, devices in straw, everlastings, appliqué work and so forth, are almost entirely old material.

The "general principles" are altogether *new*, but it is to be hoped also *true;* the rest of the book is more or less (rather more) original. The Drawings are *nearly* all fresh and with very few exceptions autograph; here and there I have pasted on to a sheet a device or monogram from the old book, but in every such case whether the plate is wholly or partly old I have withheld my signature, in all other cases my monogram is to be found on some part of the plate.

Anxious (as always) to avoid the charge of plagiarism I wish to draw special attention to plates II. and III., of which I am justly proud; and to state that they are entirely original and that they are not copied from the decorations at Grubbington-in-the-Clay (for I have never been there); but, though original, they are confessedly "very like."

I must acknowledge my indebtedness—

First to Messrs. Cox, Buckley & Co., the publishers of this book, for putting into my hands the materials on which this work is based, and for leaving "my hands free."

Secondly to Mr. Jas. Parker for the use of the figures of the nine orders of Angels on plate XIII., which are extracted from his "Calendar of the Prayer Book Illustrated."

And last but not least to my friend Mr. Brooks, who gave me the drawing of his beautiful Church at Northfleet on which to hang some garnishing, as a frontispiece to this work.

Further than this I should perhaps state that many of the Emblems in Chapter IX. are borrowed from Husenbeth's "Emblems of the Saints;" in fact the list (5) is taken bodily from that work, which indeed is a standard authority.

The same may be said of Boutell's Heraldry, which I consulted when drawing plate of the Cross. Many other books have been searched, my own sketch books among the number, and the result you have in your hands.

It is far from perfect, but I have tried to do my best, and if you, my reader, will do the same you will improve upon it, and make the Sanctuary of God each holy tide that comes

" More Glorious."

ERNEST GELDART.

Little Braxted Rectory,
    Witham,
        Trinity-tide, 1882.

DESCRIPTION OF THE PLATES.

I.

View of an Altar decorated for Christmas.

II.

Desecrated Church Furniture—Font, Pulpit, Lectern, and Altar Rails.

III.

What to avoid in decorating an Altar :—

Fig 1.—The multiplication of the Cross, unconstructional Arcading, etc.
Fig. 2.—The cumbering of the Holy Table.

IV.

A temporary Rood Screen of Lath, covered with Evergreens, etc.

V.

A side Screen to Chancel, various Wreaths, Texts, Banners, etc.

VI.

The treatment of blank Arches, Columns, and Window Sills.

VII.

Wall Diapers in Evergreens and Everlastings, etc.

VIII.

A Font decorated. 1, 2, 3, 4—Various methods of filling in plain Panels, whether of stone or wood. 5 and 6—Screen suitable either for dividing a Baptistery, or for filling in a blank Wall at the West End of a Church.

IX.

A Pulpit and two Fonts decorated.

Figs. 1—9.—Various Devices for hanging upon the Walls.
Fig. 10.—A Chancel Screen (adapted from an ancient Stone Screen).

B

X.

The Emblems of the Passion of our Redeemer.

Figs. 1—4.—The Evangelistic Symbols.
Fig. 5.—The Emblem of the Blessed Sacrament.

XI.

Various Sacred Emblems (described in the text).

XII.

The Heraldry of the Cross.

XIII.

Emblems of the Apostles and Angels, the Sacred Dove, and the Passion Flower.

XIV.

Crowns, Roses, Fleur-de-Lys, and other Emblems.

XV.

Six different Suggestions for Temporary Dossals, with Evergreens and Hangings.

XVI., XVII., AND XVIII.

Alphabets and Scroll Work.

XIX.

Texts and Illuminated Borders.

XX.

Various forms of Texts, Scrolls, and Legends for placing over Arches or on Walls.

XXI. AND XXII.

Banners and Bannerettes.

XXIII.

Various Devices in Everlasting Flowers.

XXIV.

Frame Work for Font Covers, Metal Troughs, Crosses, Flower Holders, etc., etc.

XXV.

Sketches of Frames for Screens, Patterns of "Foundations" for Devices, whether in Zinc or Card-board.

THE ART

OF

Garnishing Churches at Christmas

AND OTHER FESTIVALS.

CHAPTER I.

INTRODUCTORY.

THE "Garnishing of Churches," of which this book treats, may, now-a-days, be fairly supposed to have passed the region of apology. If argument ever was necessary to overcome prejudice or rebut objections it is so no longer. The principle of Beauty in the House of the Lord is accepted on all hands, and it is, perhaps, rather needful to temper zeal with discretion than to soften opposition.

To us of to-day, Christmas, Easter, and Whitsuntide speak so naturally from the sanctuary where " the fir tree, the pine tree, and the box together beautify the place,"* that it requires an effort of memory to recall the days when, save a few ill-set sprigs of holly at Christmas, none of these things were known.

It is then a question, rather, " *How* shall we decorate?" and not " Shall we do so?"

If indeed it is not unpleasing to God that the beautiful things of His Earth should be brought into His House, How shall they be so gathered together that " the place of His feet may be glorious?"

---

* Isaiah lx., 13.

All Church Decoration (architectural or otherwise) has a double purpose to serve—the glory of God and the edification of man. The first is secured if there be the *intention* of " an honest and good heart ; " the latter, unfortunately, cannot be, unless what is done accords with the rules of good taste.

It is probably not too much to say that, in the sight of our Maker, it matters not what materials are used or how they are disposed ; but since men are greatly influenced, for good or ill, by what they see, we must so strive to work that every touch of the chisel, every spot of colour, every line of ornament, " cry out of the wall : " that there be sermons in stones, in glass, in wood, in flowers, and fruit and leaves.

Such being the case, it is well nigh as important in temporary " Decorations," as in permanent ornament, that this end be kept in view ; that nothing may militate against the harmony of form and colour that should be found in every house, and above all in the House of Worship.

True, mistaken perpetrations in stone and wood are more serious because more enduring ; but bad taste, in however short-lived a manifestation, is, for the time being, equally painful, and if it be not too strong a word—demoralizing.

We will suppose that our readers wish to decorate a Church for one of the Festivals ; the purpose of this book is to give hints that may help them in their good endeavours. But first, a few extracts in the shape of historical notes may not be out of place.

Spenser, in his " Shepherd's Complaint," which appeared in 1579, says :

> " Youths folke now flocken in every where
> To gather May buskets and smeling breere,
> And home they hasten the posts to dight ;
> And all the Kirke pillars ere daylight
> With Hawthorne buds and sweet Eglantine
> And girlonds of Roses."

In a few words he manages to give a very complete idea of the mode in which Churches were garnished with various flowers in his day. The " posts " and pillars of the sacred building were to be decked with the fragrant blossoms of the White Thorn, with branches of Sweet Briar and garlands of Roses.

Christmas.—Stowe, in his " Survey of London," which was first published about twenty years later (1598), says :—

" Against the feast of Christmas every man's house, *as also their parish Churches*, were dressed with holme, ivy, bayes, and whatsoever the season of the year afforded to be green The conduits and standards in the streets were garnished in the same manner."

Here, again, the modern decorator may gain one or two useful hints. The quotation from old Stowe may serve to remind us that there are other available materials at Christmas besides Holly—that the Ilex or evergreen Oak, the bay, laurel, rosemary, yew, and ivy may. even in mid-winter, be used to give a festive appearance to God's house.

Perhaps óne of the most striking evidences of the antiquity of the custom is the name of the evergreen shrub Holly—evidently a corruption of " Holy." In all probability the appellation is derived from the use of holly leaves and berries to adorn Churches. The practice of decking sacred edifices with green boughs and flowers existed long before the Reformation; but it is clear that the custom was not interrupted by that event. The passages above-cited are taken from authors who wrote many years after the separation of the English Church from that of Rome, and after the revision of our Ritual and the adoption of our present Prayer-book. Several learned writers have collected interesting extracts from churchwardens' accounts in different parts of the kingdom, showing that during the sixteenth century flowers were frequently provided at the expense of the parishioners in adorning Churches.

Among the ancient annual disbursements of S. Mary-at-Hill, in the City of London, is the following entry:—" Holme and ivy at Christmas Eve, iiijd." In the churchwardens' account of S. Lawrence Parish, Reading, 1505, " It. payed to Makrell for the holy bush agayne Christmas, ijd." In similar accounts for the Parish of S. Margaret, Westminster, 1647, " Item paid for rosemarie and bayes that was stuck about the Church at Christmas, 1s, 6d."

Coles, in his " Art of Simpling," 1656, says:—" In some places setting up of holly, ivy, rosemary, bayes, yew, &c., in Churches at Christmas is still in use."

This passage, considering the date when it was written, is very remark-able. It shows that in the time of the Commonwealth, when the Puritan party was in the zenith of its power, old customs were not altogether abrogated.

In Herbert's " Country Parson " (1657, p. 56), the author tells us, " Our parson takes order that the Church be swept and kept clean without dust or cobwebs, *and at great festivals, strawed and stuck with boughs.*"

A writer in the *Gentleman's Magazine* for May, 1811, speaking of the manner in which the inhabitants of the North Riding in Yorkshire celebrate Christmas, says: " The windows and pews of the Churches (and also the windows of houses) are adorned with branches of holly, which remain till *Good Friday.*" If this were really the " use of York," it is noteworthy, as common custom fixes Candlemas Eve as the time for removal of all Christmas decorations.*

Palm Sunday.—Newton, in " Herbal for the Bible," says, speaking of the palm:—" The common people in some countries used to deck their Churches with the boughs and branches thereof, on the Sunday next before Easter." In the churchwardens' account for S. Mary Outwich, London, 1510—11, is the entry:—" First, paid for palme,† box, floures, and cakes, iiijd."

* Or Septuagesima Sunday, if that happen earlier than Feb. 2.

† Probably not real palm, but the *Salix*, or Sallow, which generally flowers towards the end of Lent.

In the accounts for All Hallows, Staining, " Item for box and palme on Palme Sundays ; item for gennepore for the Churche, ijd."

Easter.—In the churchwardens' accounts for S. Mary-at-Hill is an entry :—" Three great garlands for the crosses, of roses and lavender ; three dozen other garlands for the quire, 3s." In the churchwardens' accounts for S. Mary Outwich, London, 1525, " Paid for *brome* ageynst Easter, jd."

Whitsunday.—Collinson, in his " History of Somersetshire," speaking of the Parish of Yatton, says :—" John Lane of this parish, gent., left half an acre of ground called the ' Groves ' to the poor for ever, reserving a *quantity of grass for strewing the Church on Whitsunday.*" Among the ancient annual Church disbursements of S. Mary-at-Hill, London, is the following :—" Garlands, Whitsunday, iijd."

Harvest Festivals.—It is to be feared that the custom of decorating a Church for a Harvest Festival will have to stand on its own merits, without such witness or support as antiquity supplies in regard of the Holy Days of the Calendar.

CHAPTER II.

GENERAL PRINCIPLES.

A.—The first and most obvious principle is this—a Church when decorated should be at least as fit for use as when unadorned.

But, obvious as this would seem to be, a large proportion of the decorations commonly in vogue cumber the ground, embarrass the clergy in their ministrations, and make each recurrent festival a source of anxious foreboding. The most hopeful prospect often extends no further than a bare *chance* of being able to see the services safely through, without disturbance of the "decorations" falsely so-called ; for nothing that interferes with the use of a "garnished" place or object can rightly be said to decorate it if derivations count for anything.

It will be as well, therefore, in laying down some broad rules, to illustrate them by a few fearful examples that may show "what to avoid," and we will begin with the Font.

Since the present custom of the Church does not limit Baptism to Easter (or Whitsun) Eve, it stands to reason that a christening may occur on any day ; and, as the Prayer Book recommends " Holy days " in preference to others, a direction coincident with the natural inclination of most folk, a " Decorated " Font will in all likelihood have to be used.

But when we approach the Font, we find perhaps that the flat oak cover has been replaced by a tin trough filled with earth, and banked high with moss and flowers ; a prickly hedge surrounds it, which, on the removal of the superstructure, unwinds itself and falls to the floor, a tangled heap of brown paper, string and leaves. (See Fig. 1, Pl. II.)

Or, again, we may find a plantation of flower pots, which entirely prevents the clergyman from approaching within a foot or two of the basin.

Or else the Font (in disregard of the rubric) is found to be already full of water, stale and discoloured with decaying leaves, the result of a " floating cross " of lilies.

Surely few words are needed to show the folly of such " decorations " as these.

We will next come to the Reading Desk and Choir Stalls. Here a favourite device is to nail or glue round the *edges* of the bookboards a band of sharp leaves, which render it difficult to turn over a leaf of the Prayer Book without pricking our fingers. (Fig. 2, Pl. II.)

Another plan is to flank the *sides* of the stall ends with huge wreaths, and bunches of evergreens and flowers. These are specially perilous to the surplices of clergy and choir when they enter and leave the Chancel. (Fig. 3. Pl. II.)

The Pulpit often suffers in the same way. The preacher pricks his hands, and catches his surplice, if for a moment he forgets "where he is." There is, moreover, an additional element of danger. Unless timely warning is given by churchwarden or sacristan, the preacher may unwarily raise or lower the pulpit desk; then, as likely as not, a sharp twang of wire is heard (like the breaking of a harp string), and a shower of "all manner of things" falls down into the nave. (Fig. 4, Pl. II.) The well-meaning decorator sits below, flushing with vexation, and complains as she leaves the church—"Why couldn't Mr. Dash leave the desk alone?" To which the obvious retort would be—"Why could not Miss Blank have done so?"

The Communicants' Rail is intended to serve as a support for those who need it, either in kneeling or rising up. What, then, can be more distracting to the Communicants at the most solemn moment than to find no place to rest the hand, save a ridge of holly or a bunch of fruit. What more unseemly than to retire from the altar with patches of cotton wool clinging to the knees, or with garments stained and spoiled by crushed flowers and berries. (Figs. 7 and 8, Pl. II.)

The Altar itself is too often treated in a manner ill beseeming "God's Board." Sheaves of corn, plates of fruit, piles of grapes, hops, oats, and so forth are placed where nothing should ever be put save the bread and wine and the alms of the faithful presented at the offertory. (Fig. 1, Pl. III.)

The Lectern and Litany Desk (if there be one) suffer the fate of the Pulpit, and are dangerous and irritating to approach. (Fig. 5, Pl. II.)

It will be sufficiently clear to the reader that the foregoing remarks are based on fairly sound reasoning, and few will be found to deny that they are amply justified.

Granting, however, that nothing should interfere with the use of the Church, or its furniture, there are divers other "Cautels," and if we may so say "Prohibitions" to be laid down.

B.—Never on any account should a nail (or even a tin tack) be driven into either wood or stone.

If you cannot make a Decoration stay in its place by the law of gravitation, or by the use of string and wire, take it away and find some other place for it.

To drive nails into a rough plaster wall for the suspension of wreaths and so on is harmless, but to break the joints of a stone or marble pulpit, to riddle the edges and split the panels of oak stalls is·not *decoration* but *desecration*.

Let any one calculate the number of Festivals and the number of nails driven in each time, and it may easily be judged how long it will take before the ill-used object is completely destroyed. A century of such treatment would wreck the most substantial pulpit or font in existence.*

Another plan less destructive but almost equally disfiguring is to stick brown paper with glue or sealing wax on to the window-sills, font, pulpit, stalls, or Lectern, and upon this foundation to sew floral decorations. It should be unnecessary to remark that neither stone nor wood will endure the washing and scraping necessary for its removal without damage.

c.—No "Decoration of the Decorated" should be allowed. If gilding the refined gold be superfluous, to cover up costly carving or marble inlay with bunches of leaves is ridiculous; yet a common conception of the decoration of a stall end is to tie (or nail) on the oak "Poppy-head" a shapeless bunch of green.

A Font, if carved, should be as much as possible "left alone." If a skeleton cover of galvanized wire be put upon it wreathed with flowers, well and good; provided always that it is either easily removeable, or else that it does not hinder a Baptism. But never cover carved crochets with moss, delicate tracery with flock paper, or angels with veils of evergreen.

If, however, a Font or Pulpit be *plain* there can be no objection to wreaths and shields being suspended or tied, provided neither nails or glue be used. If it is required to garnish a Square or Octagonal Font with such devices, nothing is easier than to put a plain wire hoop upon the top from which to hang them, or to tie a cord midway for securing them. The broad rule is—Decorate plain spaces but leave details to "tell their own tale." (Figs. 11, 12, 13, Pl. IX.)

d.—Another rule is this—Never, if possible, "break the lines" of the Architecture, especially those that are *vertical*. Hence it follows that the greatest care must be taken in wreathing columns or "splining" arches.

Supposing a Church be a Norman or early Transitional building with thick short columns, heavy capitals, and square arches, it will be found that light spiral wreaths on the columns brighten them up, and that a spline covered with evergreens can be suitably bent into the square reveals of the arcade, while if the capital projects sufficiently *all round*, a thin "crown" of leaves will sit well upon it. (Fig. 1, Pl. VI.)

But the effect of treating the slender columns and the delicate arch-moulds of a late-decorated or perpendicular arcade in the same fashion is nothing short of ruinous.

e.—Never *invent* arcades or arched panels in impossible places, or on

---

* One is commonly told that *one* tin tack makes such a small hole that it is invisible. So does a drawing pin, but the corners of a drawing board are reduced to the consistency of bran in a very few years.

blank walls where there is nothing to suggest them. (Fig. 1, Pl. III.,) will probably be sufficient warning on this head.

On the other hand a plain arch may be "Cusped," or filled with tracery (Figs. 4, 5, 6, Pl. VI.), if the style of the architecture be not *violated*—as by the insertion of an Early Cusp in a Perpendicular opening, or of Geometrical tracery in a Norman arch.

It will perhaps be better to consult some one with technical knowledge before venturing on such attempts.

The same remark applies to Temporary Screens of light lath covered with foliage. (Pls. IV., V., IX.)

Nothing can be more seemly than such screens if well designed; no more admirable plan suggested than such experiments if a permanent screen be in view.

Often it is impossible to foresee the general effect, or to forecast what lines of the building it will "cut," where it will clash with some existing detail or what it will *hide*, till such a "template" is erected.

So, on the contrary, nothing will so effectually dispose of the objection frequently made by fractious churchwardens, or obstructive farmers, that "a screen" *stops the view*, and makes the Church "*look small.*"

As a general rule no screen ever does anything but make a Church look *larger*, and in nine cases out of ten, so far from *stopping* the view, it "carries it on" in a most happy manner, giving fresh beauty to what is already comely. On this head it is not beside the mark to call the reader's attention to the fact that a wild beast in the Zoological Gardens is perfectly visible though the screen of its cage is solid to the extent of nearly 50 per cent.

So it is scarcely likely that half-a-dozen uprights in a width of 15 or 20 feet will render the Chancel of a Church obscure.

F. **Never do more work than is necessary** *in the Church*, and *à fortiori* in the Chancel. Avoid, so far as possible, making the Sanctuary a workshop or a lumber-room.

If in the *unconsecrated* Temple during its building "no sound of axe or hammer" was heard, we may well think it unseemly that the sound of tools, the chatter of busy workers, and sometimes, alas, the wrangling of disputant decorators, should be heard in the Chancel of a Christian Temple. Therefore, all larger work necessitating hammering and entailing litter and rubbish should be done in the school, the vicarage, or the nearest house, and each article as it is finished brought into the Church for fixture. Or else, if there is *no* convenient place near at hand, let the vestry be used in preference to the nave, the nave or aisles in preference to the Chancel. Let all the workers honestly try to minimize the evil.

G. If it be not an impertinence, the author would humbly suggest that nothing should ever be done which is likely to arouse prejudice without good cause. If, for example, it is *known* that half-a-dozen people will be troubled in mind by some emblem or text likely to be *misconstrued*, and which has no *necessary* bearing on the Feast or its services, charity, not to say prudence, would suggest the substitution of some other ornament.

At the same time it must be admitted that no amount of forethought can ensure immunity from offence. The Churchwarden who saw the sacred monogram ☧ and complained of the excess of Popery, which, unsatisfied with Pius ✗ IX, demanded Pius X, is, after all, but typical.

H. As far as possible avoid *sameness* and feeble repetition. If the hoops or wire frames used at one festival are again employed, try to vary their *position* as well as their vegetable or other covering.

Who does not know the weary anticipation which awaits the re-appearance of a well-known interlaced triangle or vesica, or S. Andrew Cross, covered with blue flannel at Christmas, white at Easter, and red at Pentecost; or of a dingy "Ter-Sanctus," recurring with unfailing regularity upon the altar or screen? A little ingenuity, a little extra thought would prevent such distasteful monotony.

I. Avoid meaningless multiplication of symbols and emblems.

If a Church is dedicated to S. Peter, do not let the cross keys meet the eye at every turn; if to S. Andrew, let the ✗ cross be varied by *something* else. There are few saints but have two or more emblems.

So with the cross of Christ the most sacred, yet, at the same time, the most vulgar of ornaments. Far too often it is used simply as a *dernier ressort* when invention fails. "Oh, put a cross," is an easy solution of a difficulty; but it is not reverent nor is it edifying to see the symbol of redemption scattered broadcast. Specially should this be borne in mind on the Altar. If there is one cross upon the ledge no other is needed. Fig. 1 Pl. III., which is little if anything exaggerated, shows the length to which this evil will run.

K. Never put cut flowers in places where they will wither, unless they are easily accessible, and can be renewed; else before the "Octave" of Easter or Whitsunday is past they will be a sorry spectacle, and unsavory withal.

Whenever possible try to contrive that they may stand in water. Narrow zinc troughs, made to fit the window sills; little "cones" for bunches of choicer flowers are not expensive, and even if they were would be well worth their cost. (See Pl. XXIV.) Growing flowers or even small shrubs in pots may fitly be introduced in larger Churches; either standing on the floor, in niches, or on wall brackets where they exist.

L. Let there be a due proportion, "The better the day the better the deed." Do not let the great festivals of our blessed Lord be overshadowed by some local feast as a village anniversary or a harvest festival.

So, too, on each several feast let the same principle be kept in view. As each part of the sacred building has its use let it be garnished suitably and with due regard to the other parts.

Do not let the less sacred be more ornate than the more holy. Let the Porch lead to the Nave, the Nave to the Chancel, and that to the Sanctuary or the Eastern End. So with regard to the architecture, small aisles or transepts should not distract attention from the central line of the building.

So, too, with regard to the designs used. One should not by its discord or strong colouring throw another into the shade. There should be, in a word, unity of plan and harmony of detail. As Ruskin, in his " Seven Lamps of Architecture," observes—" Our building, if it is well composed, is one thing, and is to be coloured as Nature would colour one thing—a shell, a flower, or an animal ; not as she colours groups of things."

M. Lastly, before entering upon details, it is advisable to suggest the desirability of making all the arrangements in good time, and for this purpose a meeting of those interested in the decorations should be called some weeks before Christmas or Easter to arrange a definite scheme on which to proceed ; and, if possible, a leader should be appointed, whose opinion should be final on all matters of detail.

It is also desirable to give members of the congregation the opportunity of contributing towards the decorations. This can be done either by a notice saying to whom contributions may be sent, or by having a box to receive them placed in the Church.

As soon as the general plan and details have been decided upon, whatever devices, banners, texts, or other materials are required should be ordered from the decorator, so as to prevent the possibility of delay occurring.

" LET ALL THINGS BE DONE DECENTLY AND IN ORDER."

CHAPTER III.

On the Making of Wreaths and Other Floral Ornaments.

In all Churches, whether more or less elaborately decorated, wreaths are the staple garniture; therefore a few hints on the various ways in which they may be arranged, and the mode of constructing them, will no doubt be acceptable. Large boughs, to cut which would injure the trees, are not required; only small pieces, such as the gardeners when trimming would throw away, are wanted, as these only can be used to produce the effect desired. Almost all evergreens are suitable; but holly, by custom and by its association, should be extensively used at Christmas and all other winter festivals; as the lovely white hawthorn should be used on the feast day of SS. Philip and James, or other spring festivals. Ivy, yew, fir, and box will also be found very useful. In many positions the long runners of ivy, thickened out by extra leaves being wired on, will produce a good effect and be quickly made.

The more usual plan is to fasten the evergreens with twine to a thin rope; and the most convenient and expeditious plan to adopt is to have the rope of the necessary length, stretched across the room at a convenient height (say rather more than three feet from the floor), and to have a quantity of evergreen sprigs assorted in heaps of different kinds, also a supply of small bunches of holly berries, and (if it is intended to use them) of everlasting flowers, arranged on a table close at hand. Begin by disposing a few of the sprigs round the rope, and fasten them on with twine; arrange the next bunch so that the stalks may not be seen, and twist the string round them, tying a knot to prevent its slipping away. This should be continued until the rope is covered; and care should be taken to use, as far as possible, a variety of tints of green, interspersed with bunches of holly berries and everlastings, as also to keep the thickness of the wreath uniform. The bunches of holly berries, if large, may be divided by splitting them through the stalks. It is desirable to wear gloves to protect the hands when making holly wreaths.

There is one objection to the use of twine for fastening the evergreens to the rope in the way described above, viz., that unless it is frequently looped or tied, as well as wound round the twigs of which the wreath is formed, they are apt to get disarranged in moving and fixing, by the twine slipping. This can be avoided by using either fine iron or copper wire in lieu of twine ; the wire will bend with the wreaths, and consequently not allow the evergreens to get misplaced.

Another plan is to make the wreaths flat instead of round ; the best way of accomplishing this is to use a stout string or whipcord, instead of a rope foundation—to have twigs cut with rather longer stalks than usual, and to fasten them with wire in the way described above ; but arranging the various pieces spreading out instead of bound close to the string ; when arranged in this way, care should be taken that the choicest pieces are placed so as to show well on the face of this flat wreath.

A wreath made in this manner is more pliable, and consequently, for some parts of the work, more easily arranged than when so thick a foundation as rope is used ; but it must not be forgotten that massive pillars require much thicker wreaths than those of lighter proportions ; and care must be taken that all the leaves, &c., are directed upwards. This is a point that should be constantly kept in mind, as frequent mistakes are made in the matter.

An amateur, who has had great experience in Church decorations, has kindly given a description of the method which he employs for wreath-making.

This gentleman considers that it is far preferable to use a stout wire as the ground whereon to fasten the wreath, and fine brass wire for binding on the foliage, &c. He uses the wire over his knees, having the uncovered part on the left side and the completed work falling to the right. In this way as much as 100 feet may be made in a length, and the everlastings, or anything else that may be wished to be interwoven with the wreath, can be inserted as the work progresses. In this manner a wreath can be made either very fine, as of a single spray of box, or very thick, according to the purpose for which it is required.

The following plan of constructing the wreaths will perhaps be found to be more easily worked by ladies than either of the foregoing, and quite as effective :—Instead of the wire or cord groundwork, procure some green worsted binding, and stretch it tight across a table, and then sew thereon the twigs, flowers, and berries, arranged in the same way as previously described. This will give a rather broad and flat wreath, which will look very well, particularly when used for decorating large columns.

Wire ribbon, i.e., a wire foundation, covered with cotton, can be procured, either black or white, and this makes a capital foundation for wreaths, as the leaves can be sewn on in the same way as on to worsted binding.

For wreaths to fit into the carved mouldings of an arcade, the best groundwork is a thin wooden lath, which, if cut to the exact length required, will, when decorated and put into its position, require no fastening, as the natural spring of the wood will keep it in its place. A thin iron rod treated in the same manner can be bent to the required shape, and would answer equally well. In fixing wreaths, and in fact all temporary decorations, it is of the greatest importance to use as few nails as possible, and where used they should be put in with the greatest care, as it is most unsightly when the decorations are taken down, to leave the plaster, or brickwork, disfigured. It is to be hoped that enough has been said already on the question of stone and wood-work to render any further remarks here unnecessary. One only exception to the rule which defends wood from nails, may perhaps be fairly made in the matter of beams and rafters, if for instance, in a village Church there are large beams crossing the nave at the wall-plate, it may not be found a bad plan to drive in large nails at regular intervals for the hanging of evergreen wreaths and *leave* them there. Thus—

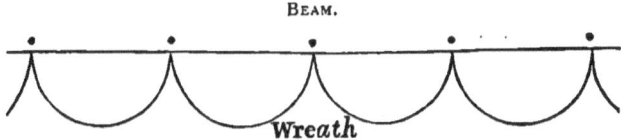

In many positions a thin wire hook or staple, such as is used by bell-hangers, can be driven into the walls without doing any damage, and these will often be found to be convenient for fixing the wreaths or devices. For minute work, such as fonts, &c., moss wreaths are suitable, as they are very pliant.

So it is a good plan to leave a few nails, staples, or whatever is used for fixing the decorations, in places where they are *always required* when the building is decorated; as, if small, and at a height from the ground, they would not be observed. For wreaths round the capitals of columns, it is found to be a good plan to use a band of hoop iron with a hole punched in each end. This forms the groundwork for the wreath, and is bent to encircle the column. The ends are then fastened by a piece of string or wire. A better plan is to have the hoop iron, above described, fastened in the centre of a band of per-forated zinc about three inches wide. This will enable a breadth to be given to the wreath which its position requires. Where there is a projected moulding on which this band can rest, no other fastening is required; but where this is not the case it is better to have a hole punched in the centre of the hoop iron as well as at the ends, so that it can be fastened on each side by a piece of string, which should be tied round the column.

A flexible wreath hanging freely suspended from two points assumes, by its own weight, the curve which mathematicians call the *catenary*. It is one of the most beautiful curves in nature, as any one will acknowledge who has observed the graceful droop of the chains of a suspension-bridge, or, on a smaller scale, of a cord hanging between two points, and not *taut*. The catenary is capable also of great variety. The droop may be very small com-pared with the horizontal span, so that the curve is flat and open: or, on the other hand, it may hang down so as to present the form of a narrow pendant loop. When the wreath is ready, all that remains to be done is to hang it over the points of suspension. No framework is needed, and the form naturally assumed is one which art would not improve.

Perhaps one of the very simplest and most easily-constructed kinds of decoration is a horizontal series of plain and equal festoons : this may be continued all round the nave, either above the windows of the aisles, or the interior arches—or both.

Another form of festoons, slightly more complicated, is that of a double series intersecting each other as in the annexed diagram—

Another variation of the same idea consists of a series of festoons, one under the other ; the summits of the lower series of curves being coincident with the lowest points of the upper series—

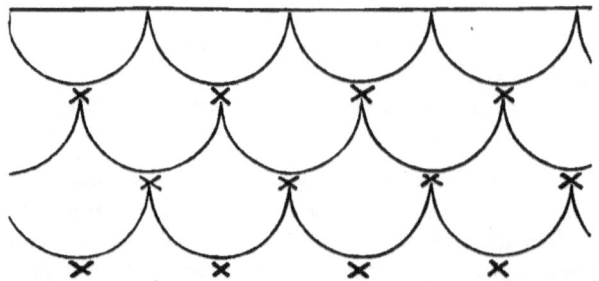

Such a treatment is suitable for large blank *brick* walls if time and materials sufficient are forthcoming. If wreaths of this sort be used, the courses of the brick work give place for the nails (which need only be small), and if at **XX** small bunches of white or yellow everlastings be placed, the effect will be very bright and happy.

CHAPTER IV.

DEVICES IN EVERGREENS.

For forming devices, either entirely of evergreens, or of evergreens with the addition of a few everlasting flowers, perforated zinc* is perhaps the best ground-work. The plan to be adopted for fixing them is as follows :—First procure the materials required, viz., the devices proposed to be decorated, cut out in perforated zinc, a supply of evergreen leaves, and very small sprays of evergreens, some stout needles, and strong thread of a dark colour—that used for sewing carpets or ordinary black thread will do.

Commence sewing on the leaves and sprays at the bottom of the device, taking care that the thread fastens the leaves down across one of the veins, and that the stalks are as far as possible covered by other leaves. For devices that are intended to be fixed at a slight elevation, small leaves should be used, and the work should be done as neatly as possible ; but for those that are to be fixed at a considerable height, larger leaves will be more effective. Devices consisting entirely of evergreens have a somewhat heavy appearance, which is greatly relieved by small bunches either of holly berries, or of the coloured everlasting flowers being introduced in different parts of the design, in the way indicated on some of the illustrations in this book, and described in the next Section.

Those who have a knowledge of drawing will find it best to make a sketch of the device in the first instance, and then with a little colour, to ascertain in what position it will be best to introduce the flowers. Very effective devices can be formed by having the centre illuminated in colours, and the outer part formed in evergreens.

Another plan for forming the devices in evergreens is to have a ground-work of stout iron wire, which is, of course, less expensive. The leaves can be either tied on with thread, or better, bound on with the fine wire used by artificial flower makers. The wire groundwork, however, does not give the same breadth to the design, and the leaves cannot be arranged so well, except in the case of

---

* Or galvanized iron wire or hoop, made to the required shape.

D

very large devices, where the leaves could be attached by the stalks to the wire frame in such a way as to spread out.

Where devices are fixed against the light as in the case of a temporary (and tentative) Dossal, which comes above the ledge of the east window, it will be requsite to stop all light passing through, as, if this is not done, the effect will be considerably spoiled. As good a manner as any of doing this is to fasten some waterproofed paper at the back ; this can be procured at 2d. per yard and is impervious to light. See Figs. 1—9, Pl. IX., Figs. 2, 3, Pl XV.

CHAPTER V.

Devices in Everlasting Flowers, Berries, and Moss.

For working with the everlasting flowers most people prefer a ground-work of perforated zinc cut out to the required shape, as the stalks can be put through the holes and fastened behind either with cotton, or by pasting or glueing stout brown paper over the back. Another plan is to have the ground-work shaped out of cardboard or of a thin piece of wood, which should be either covered with paper or painted, and on this the flowers, cut from the stalks, are fastened down either with glue, very thick gum, or shoemakers' paste.

Melted gelatine will be found more useful than gum arabic for fixing the flowers and berries. The gelatine can be spread over the device, and the flowers laid on ; but for berries it is best to dip them in a saucer containing the gelatine.

Supposing either of the above plans to be adopted, the worker should procure the device selected, cut out to the required size, and then lay it down on a piece of plain paper, and with a pencil trace the shape. Then remove the zinc, and with water-colours try the effect of the various shades it is proposed to use ; for it should always be borne in mind that it is *not* requisite to adhere to one colour only with these flower decorations. Thus, a star, instead of being all yellow, may have the principal part yellow, with a green centre, and a line of red around the outside edge.

A double triangle may have one yellow, edged with red, and the other white, edged with blue. The designs given on Plate XXIII. indicate this arrangement.

By trying the effect on paper in the way suggested, one is much more likely to get a satisfactory result, and it will also save time in arranging the flowers.

The *gnaphaliums* can be procured in the following colours :—

Yellow,	Lilac,	Spotted Red,
White,	Pink,	Blue,
Green,	Orange or Light Red,	Violet,
Spotted Yellow,	Black,	Purple,
Crimson,		

as well as some others. It should be remembered that they are real flowers dried (and in some cases dyed), not artificial, as some people erroneously imagine.

The larger varieties of everlasting flowers *(helichrysum)* are grown in several colours, and these are used in conjunction with the *gnaphaliums* with very good effect, but not alone.

White Cape Everlastings are very effective for decorations. Before use, the seed in the centre should be removed, and they should be warmed by steam or in front of a fire, opened out flat, and turned face downwards, leaving the back uppermost. When used in this way, a comparatively small number are required. They are also used the other way, much closer together. The Cape silver leaves are also very effective.

There are also many very beautiful *grasses*, too often disfigured by being dyed bright blue or red, but easily to be obtained *au naturel*; these are useful and legitimate substitutes for flowers in the winter season, and may even be placed in vases on the altar without incongruity.

NATURAL FLOWERS.

Where real flowers are used, arrangements must of course be made for the stalks to be kept moist, and this can very easily be done by water contained in little zinc tubes, which can be soldered in any position on to an iron frame bent to the required form ; or these zinc tubes (formed as cones, and made with a hook) can be hung on to any part of the decorations required. A drop of thin gum in each of the flowers will prevent them falling to pieces as soon as they otherwise would. The stalks also can be dipped in hot sealing-wax. For flower vases a useful frame is made in zinc, which enables the decorator to make an effective bouquet with a small supply of flowers ; an illustration of this and of other useful contrivances for similar purposes will be found on Plate XXIV. Primroses for Easter decorations can be kept very well by having the stalks stuck in wet clay.

In some positions, as for instance round the base of the font, the best plan to adopt is to have troughs of zinc, to hold the water, and to have floating in them boards perforated with holes ; these can be covered with moss, and the stalks of the flowers passed through the holes to the water.

When flowers in pots are used, a convenient and effective plan is to place them in hanging wall baskets, concealing the pots with moss, or to place them upon brackets as already described in Ch. II.

CHAPTER VI.

Illuminated and other Devices.

These can be prepared either in oil or water-colours, on cardboard, calico, or prepared cloth. The device should either be procured from the decorator, set out ready for illumination, or a full-sized drawing should be made, and then traced upon the substance to be illuminated. The best way of tracing it is to prick holes all round the outline, and then lay it down on the prepared cloth or other material, and with a little whitening*, tied up in a piece of muslin, dust it over. On removing the drawing it will be found that the whitening, which has passed through the pin holes, will show the outline, which will enable the worker to sketch the device easily with a black-lead pencil or chalk. When this has been done, the colours and gold should be filled in in the same manner as described in Chapter VIII. for illuminating texts.

Most monograms and devices look well when surrounded by a wreath, composed either of evergreens or of everlasting flowers, or of the two combined. See Figs. on Pl. 9, etc.

An easy way of preparing effective devices with an illuminated centre and a flower and evergreen border, is to procure the device cut out in perforated zinc, and fix the illumination painted on prepared cloth in the centre, and then surround it with flowers or evergreens.

A simple and effective way of forming devices is to sketch out with a black-lead pencil, on either prepared calico or cardboard, the outline of the monograms, crosses, or other ornaments selected, and then fill them in with a rich deep red in oil colour. This on the white ground, surrounded with a wreath of evergreens, interspersed with everlasting flowers and berries, will be found to have a very pleasing appearance. The monograms and crosses shown on Plates XI., XII., XIII. are suitable for this purpose.

A great variety of designs for illuminated monograms, crosses, and devices are given in the illustrations.

---

* Or if the *ground* be white, powdered " blue," or brick-dust beaten fine in a mortar will serve equally well.

Rice Devices.—Letters and devices can be formed by having cut out cardboard patterns, and having steeped some gum tragacanth in water to a jelly, putting a layer of large Carolina rice on the pattern with it, and when dry, adding another layer, and so on as required. They can either be left white, or coated red with sealing wax dissolved in spirits of wine.

Appliqué,

Of which we have no thoroughly English synonym—is used to express the art of laying one material upon another to form a pattern, figure, or any other work that may be desired.

It will thus be seen that "appliqué work" opens a large field for the display of taste and ingenuity, especially by the lady decorator, as it embraces work in almost every conceivable material, from coloured paper to the richest silk, velvet, or even cloth of gold. As Mulready, when asked the secret of his great success in colouring his pictures, said, " Know what you have to do," so we say, the great object of the amateur decorator should be to secure unity— i.e., to make out of many things one perfect whole. And the first thing is to have the required device set out in full size ready for working, and to decide upon the materials and colours of the various parts.

To enable such of our readers as would wish to apply themselves to this appliqué work to prepare the materials selected for the purpose, we cannot do better than give the following extract from "Church Embroidery," by Mrs. Dolby:—

" To Prepare Velvet, Cloth, and Cloths of Gold and Silver for Appliqué.

" Strain a piece of rather thin holland of about 1s. per yard—*not Union*—tightly in a frame, and cover it all over with ' Embroidery Paste,' carefully removing even the most minute lump from the surface. Upon this pasted holland, while wet, lay the piece of velvet or other material of which the appliqué is to be, smoothing it over the holland with a soft handkerchief, to secure its even adhesion everywhere. If there be a necessity for drying quickly, place the frame upright at a distance of four feet from the fire, holland side to the stove. But it is always best, if possible, to *prepare* the material the day before using, that it may dry naturally, the action of the fire being likely to injure some fabrics as well as colours. The velvet, when perfectly dry, will be found tenaciously fixed to the holland, and may be removed from the frame.

" Now the entire design, or that portion of it intended to be formed of this material, is to be pounced through its pricked pattern on the holland side of the velvet, and traced correctly with a soft black-lead pencil; then cut out with sharp strong nail scissors, and it will be ready for applying to the article it is designed to ornament."

The embroidery paste alluded to is made in the following manner :— Take three table-spoonfuls of flour, and as much powdered resin as will lie on a shilling ; mix them smoothly with half a pint of water, pour into an iron saucepan, and stir till it boils. Let it boil five minutes; then turn it into a basin, and when quite cold it is fit for use.

If the device is intended to be worked upon velvet, cloth or other material, the groundwork should be stretched upon a frame, and the ornaments, prepared in the way described, tacked thereon in their proper positions. This, of course, requires great care, so that the ornaments or letters may be all straight and symmetrical : for as one false note spoils the melody of a song, so one ornament or letter not properly in harmony with the others will spoil the effect of decoration. All the ornaments having been tacked on and ascertained to be in their proper places, they should be sewn on and edged with an outline of dark cord ; or if the ornaments should be of a dark colour, with tracing braid, either white, gold colour, or red and gold, as will best contrast with the work.

If, however, the device is formed of coloured paper, all that it is necessary to do is to cut out the various parts or pieces in the desired tints, and paste them on the groundwork.

In all cases a dark line should be run round the ornament.

Much labour is thrown away, however, in forming devices or texts in coloured paper, as they have always a very meagre look ; and the same time devoted to them on painted or prepared cloth would produce a work of a much better sort.

BANNERS.

These are often made of paper or calico, and when of small size and simple design, they look sufficiently well. They can be hung at intervals beneath the cornice of the aisle roofs, or in the spandrels of the arcades ; but it should be borne in mind that good rich flags of silk or cloth, are suitable objects to hang at any time on the walls of the sanctuary ; and as they can easily be worked by amateurs, or bought at the ecclesiastical warehouse, it is better to have a few such banners in addition to the smaller bannerettes.

If possible, actual embroidery of needlework should form their ornament, but if that be found too costly, *appliqué* work should at least be used. On Plates XXI. and XXII. some 40 designs are given, and several appear on other plates.

STRAW DEVICES.

There are several different ways in which straw can be applied to decorations. The easiest, and at the same time the most effective plan, is to use the straw tissue which can be procured in sheets 17 inches + 6¼ inches or 21 inches +8¼ inches. The letters or devices are then cut out to the required size and mounted on the groundwork with thin glue. A coloured flock-paper or cotton-velvet ground, with inscription or ornament in straw tissue is very effective. Another plan is to use the straw plaits which can be procured in hanks of long lengths and various widths; but care should be taken to get a good pliable quality, as most sorts are brittle, and crack or break when bent about much.

The letters or devices to be formed with these plaits should be first cut out in cardboard, and then the straw sewn on to them. The straw can be applied either flat or in high relief, according to the taste or skill of the decorator.

A third plan of working in straw is to procure whole straws, sold in bundles, and to split them with a small tool which is made for the purpose, and with these to form the required design.

CHAPTER VII.

Wall Diapers, Temporary Screens, etc.

A wide and legitimate field is often open to the decorator at the east end of the chancel and other large wall spaces.

" Wall diapers," formed of evergreens and flowers, may well be placed against the east end of the chancel, either on the north and south sides of the altar (with a temporary reredos over it), or else covering the whole of the east wall to any height that may be convenient. See Plates I., VII., VIII. and XV.

These Diapers can be made either entirely of stout iron wire, or a combination of wooden laths, or strips of perforated zinc and wire. An infinite variety of designs can be arranged in this manner from the simple lattice to the most elaborate set patterns, filled with emblems and devices.

Those of a simple character look very well if laid on a groundwork of the white buckram calico. For others, more elaborate, unglazed cotton of various colours can be used, either with or without the white, to vary the background, according to the requirements of the design.

For diapers of an elaborate character the whole of the groundwork could be cut out of sheets of perforated zinc, and on this material they can be more readily worked, and more easily fixed. Effective wall diapers can also be made by having the simple lattice pattern very open, covering it with evergreens, and illuminating, in oil colours or gold, small ornamental devices on the groundwork. When there is no reredos, an effective dossal can be formed, either in stuff with ornaments in appliqué, or in calico or prepared cloth, illuminated. See Plate XV.

A temporary screen, as has already been said, affords a very good opportunity of trying the effect of a more lasting structure.

A few upright posts (say 2 inches × 1 inch), a cross beam of the same thickness, a few laths and barrel hoops are all the materials necessary for its construction, and with the expenditure of a little time and trouble, a really architectural effect may easily be obtained. The arches are formed by segments

E

of the barrel hoops, and the inner cusps* are made by cutting a thin hoop half through, and then bending it backwards Ɛ thus.

The whole can be covered with moss and box, or other evergreens, taking care that the uprights are kept square and trim, with no loose sprigs projecting. Crockets, bases, capitals and mid-bands can fairly be represented by small bunches of foliage, flowers or berries. The lower part or "wall" of the screen had better be filled in "solid," with serge, cotton twill, or any other suitable fabric, divided into panels with strips of evergreen. Screens of this kind may be placed both across the chancel arch and on either side of the choir, if openings exist.

The various plates on which such screens are drawn will doubtless serve as sufficiently suggestive of what may be done in this direction.

TEMPORARY DOSSALS.

On Plate XV. six examples of such decorations are given, a brief description of which may, perhaps, be required; as it is impossible for an uncoloured drawing to speak for itself in such matters.

I. Shows a Dossal of evergreen framework, the background being made of serge cotton twill, or any other fabric, white or coloured. The cross and monogram are cut out in stout cardboard and covered with coloured paper or holly berries, or everlastings, or "straw tissue." The side curtains are of serge, lightly embroidered in crewel or other work.

II. Shows a "Reredos" of a more ambitious nature, made in lath or wire work (as before described under the heading of Screens), the panels being painted by hand. This is intended to act as a "template" for a permanent Reredos; so that from this experiment one may judge whether height and shape suit the Church.

III. Is also executed in lath work, the whole background filled in with serge or cotton (as above) in different colours, the text on cartridge paper or prepared cloth.

IV. Is the same, except that the panels of the "Reredos" are filled in with painted devices.

V. Shows a dossal cloth, either worked by hand or woven, the side wings being of lath work and cotton twill. For the lower "dado" use a dark shade, say of maroon red, and powder it either with devices in everlasting flowers, or with fleur-de-lys, or quartrefoils, or roses, cut out in cardboard

---

* Greater "truth" in the curves can be obtained by having the cusps and finer tracery made of stout galvanized wire or hoop iron.

and painted. The window ledge is banked up with evergreens neatly packed and two pots of flowers marking the ends of the Dossal.

VI. Is of a more permanent character, being (save the text) altogether executed in tapestry or embroidery.

The writer has thought it needless to multiply examples, for the many designs of wall diapers, shown on the plates, may all be worked in for such purposes. Those on Plate VII., for instance, are simply shown under an arcade for the sake of making the designs hang together.

CHAPTER VIII.

TEXTS.

The 82nd Canon of 1603, among other directions, requires that there be "chosen sentences written upon the walls of churches in places convenient."

Appropriate texts and legends are among the most effective of festival decorations; as also they are valuable "silent preachers," in the more permanent form contemplated by the framers of the Canon.

The best known of these is the Decalogue which, with the Creed and Lord's Prayer, was formerly of almost universal occurrence in Parish Churches, but not in Cathedrals or Collegiate Churches. The reason of this is clear. In days when *books* were scarcer even than *readers*, it was most convenient that those things which "every Christian should know for his soul's health" should be ever before his eyes. Until a comparatively recent date these sentences were boldly printed in black and white, and were *legible*.

In the earlier days of the tractarian and ecclesiological movement, many people failing to find ancient precedent for this custom, framed the commandments in a "reredos," and by dint of illumination and "compression" made them as good (or bad) as non-existant.

In the next stage of architectural progress the commandments were banished, and at the present time but a small percentage of new or restored churches possess them.

The argument against them is (*a*) they are not mediæval, and consequently if over the altar they are out of accord with a Gothic reredos. (*b*) They are no longer needed since all men have books.

But on the other hand while they are ordered by the Canon, it is perhaps hardly wise to omit them, and there is certainly one very appropriate position which they may well occupy, *i.e.*, in that part of the Church where the *children* sit, be it west or east. There is a special fitness moreover if they are put near the font, so that the prayer, faith and obedience of the baptized may stand to them as a constant reminder of their Christian profession.

Beyond these well-known "texts" there are many others which are equally suitable for temporary or lasting decoration. Any one of the canticles may be written continuously round the walls or on the cornice; the *Benedictus* or *Magnificat*, the *Benedicite* or *Te Deum* will never weary the eye or heart of the reader.

So for a Harvest Festival the Psalm *Jubilate* may be divided into short verses and placed in the window sills round the church, so too with Pls. cxlvii., cxlviii., cl.

Or in Lent the *Miserere* or *De profundis* may be used in the same way.

Shorter texts (or even single words) may be placed on scrolls or in panels edged with foliage, and placed over doorways, at the sides of the east window, over the altar or at the entrance to the chancel, or shields " inscribed " may be hung on the walls in the spandrels of an arcade or sometimes on the columns themselves, if they be very solid or square.

It is a question, not lightly to be settled or taken as universally applicable, whether these texts should be in Latin or English, and whether (whichever tongue is chosen) they should be written in Roman or Gothic lettering.

Possibly it may be thought to be unadvisable to employ aught but English in country places, while Latin *may* be used in town. This point the writer will not attempt to discuss.

As to the condemnation of the Gothic character on the score of illegibility, it should be remembered that a large number of titles and headings in ordinary books and newspapers* are so written, that there is certainly not a railway station or hoarding but has several such inscriptions in the way of advertisement ; and as there is no question of which is the more beautiful, it seems a pity to throw away the old text, and by so doing render its chances of survival smaller.

Suppose, however, a mission room in London with nothing ecclesiastical in its form or furniture save the altar, there, without question, good bold roman type will tell the tale most readily.

There are various modes of forming texts for temporary decorations.

The plan usually adopted by amateurs as the simplest, is to cut the letters out in coloured paper, and gum or paste them on a groundwork of plain or different coloured paper or cloth.

In order to form the letters well, it is best to procure an alphabet cut out in cardboard to the required size ; and by laying the letters down on the paper, and running a line round them, the proper shape will be obtained, when they

---

* It may interest the reader to know that the following newspaper headings contain the *whole alphabet* from a to z.—Morning Post, Daily News, Queen, Field, Exchange and Mart, John Bull, East Kent Advertizer.

can be cut out with either a knife or a pair of scissors. Letters printed on paper can also be procured; these will save a good deal of time, and insure their being of the right shape.

When the letters have been cut out, they should be fixed on the ground-work that has been prepared for them.

In order that texts may look well, it is absolutely essential that all the letters should be upright and properly spaced out; and to insure this, the material on which the letters are to be fixed should be arranged on any long bench or table—a school desk for instance will serve very well.

The letters should *all* be laid out in their proper places before any of them are fastened down. It is a good plan to rule a few pencil lines at the top and bottom of the letters; and in fixing them, to insure their being upright, either to use a T or set square, or what will answer as well, a square piece of cardboard laid on the pencil line, so that its edge will give a right angle. The necessity of keeping the letters both upright and equidistant must be strongly urged. It frequently occurs that decorations, which have evidently cost much time and attention, are completely spoiled by want of regularity.

After the letters have been fixed on the groundwork they should be surrounded by a border. This may be made either of evergreens, with ever-lasting flowers introduced in the manner described on another page, or the text may be first surrounded with a border cut out of coloured papers, and then may have an outer border of evergreens, &c., beyond the coloured one. See Plate XIX.

Another plan is to procure borders painted on strips of buckram calico; these can be used for the same purpose, and admit of a great variety of designs being used.

Where paper texts, as above described, are not considered sufficiently rich in appearance, the following more elaborate plan is suggested:—Procure some white glazed buckram calico, and cut it to the required size (if fastened on a board, so much the better), then take pieces of coloured cloth, or what is better, cotton velvet, of the colour preferred, and cut the letters and borders from them in the same manner as directed for paper texts, then paste or glue them to the calico or other groundwork, surrounding the whole with borders prepared in the manner indicated above. The embroidery paste, a receipt for which is given on page 30, is the best material to use for the purpose.

Very effective texts may be prepared by covering a board with green leaves, and then forming letters upon them in white cotton wool. Great care, however, must be taken, if this plan is adopted, to get the letters quite even, as, owing to the nature of the materials, it is somewhat difficult. The letters should first be cut in cardboard, then the cotton wool put on and cut to shape; if sprinkled with "crystal frost," the appearance is greatly improved.

Another way is to prepare the board with evergreens as above described, and form the text with roses, camellias, or any other flowers which can be procured, so that the principal letters might be red, the remainder white ; in the same manner that red and black are used in illuminating decorations in oil colours.

A plan frequently adopted is to cover cardboard letters with evergreens, and fasten them to the wall separately ; but the objection to this plan is, that there is a great risk of defacing the plaster by the number of tacks or nails that would have to be used in fixing. The better plan is to use a board that has been covered with white or coloured paper, and then, when the letters have been put on, to surround the whole with a narrow border, consisting of small sprigs of box or other evergreens, of which the leaves are quite small. The advantage obtained by this plan is, that the board can then be suspended in the required position upon two nails, which, besides avoiding the risk of injury to the walls above alluded to, also saves a great deal of time and trouble in fixing.

The various methods above described for making texts are all applications of the principle of cutting out one material and laying it on another ; but where the aid of painting is attainable, a much larger field is open, and greater variety of treatment, both as regards design and colour.

For those who have not had much experience in illuminated decorations, it is best to procure pots of colours already prepared for use, which can be thinned with a little turpentine if found to be too thick.

The best groundwork for these decorations is " prepared cloth," a material which is painted and prepared for decoration in the same way as canvas for oil painting.

Decorations done on prepared cloth, if carefully rolled round wooden rollers when put away, will last for years.

When a cheaper material is required, white glazed buckram calico can be used, the process of painting being the same as on the prepared cloth.

When the material on which the text is to be written has been extended on a board or table, and the text spaced out, so as to obtain the proper distances between each word, the cardboard letter previously described should be laid upon it, and marked out with a black-lead pencil, care being taken to get a clear and distinct outline, and to keep the letters regular.

This being done, the next process is to fill in all the letters with their proper colours, using a camel hair, or sable brush, and putting only enough paint to cover the groundwork.

Should any of the letters or ornament be required to be gilt, the leaf gold is the best to be used, and the most durable. It is sold in books, and in order to apply it properly, a gilder's cushion, knife, and brush are required, as well as gold size. The gold size should be laid on the parts to be gilt, and when it is *almost* dry, it should be breathed upon to ensure its being sufficiently "sticky," then lay out a leaf of gold on the cushion and cut it with the knife to the required size. This should be taken up with the gilder's brush and applied, care being taken that the parts are well covered with the leaf; then rub them gently over with a piece of cotton wool to remove all superfluous gold. An outline of black or red round the gold greatly improves the appearance of the gilded letters or ornament. "Transfer gold leaf" has been lately introduced, specially for amateurs' use; it is mounted on paper and can be cut with scissors to the required size. The work to be gilt is sized in the usual way, and the sheet laid upon it; the paper will peel off and leave the gold.

If the texts are not intended to be kept from year to year, and gold leaf is considered either too expensive or too troublesome to be used, bronze powder can be substituted. The work should be prepared with gold size in the way before described, and the powder, which will only adhere to the parts sized, may then be dusted on.

Where gold leaf is used, a good effect is produced by having a shaped patch at the commencement of the text, on which to place its initial letter; and the introduction of some fine lines of ornament, in the style adopted in the old illuminated missals, will still further enrich it.

A new material for decoration has been introduced during the last few years, called crystal frost. This is made of crystal glass, which, in its molten state, possesses great ductility. When in this state it is blown into exceedingly thin globules, which immediately burst and produce the frost.

It can be used in a variety of decorations, and will adhere, without any preparation, to silk, paper, &c. The best way of applying it, however, is to use a little clear liquid gum; but the smallest possible quantity of gum should be used, and the "frost" not applied till it is *nearly* dry, only *just* sticky. Another very effective material is the "Gold Metal" Powder, which is applied in the same way as the "frost," saving that the size should be much stronger.

Letters or devices cut in cardboard or paper, and covered with the crystal frost, if placed on a dark coloured groundwork of either cotton velvet, cloth, or calico, are very brilliant.

STRAW TISSUE.—This material is very effective, and is the most easily worked of any of the methods of using straw. It is sold in sheets, and consists of split straws mounted on a paper backing and rolled flat by machinery. Any texts or devices can easily be cut in this with a knife, and when mounted on flock-paper or other dark background, produce a telling effect with very little trouble. When large devices are required, the sheets can be joined, and when up, the joints will hardly be noticed. Glue or paste is the best material for mounting the straw tissue with, and a heavy weight should be placed on it till it is dry. Letters and devices can be procured cut out in straw tissue ready for mounting. A greatly improved effect is gained by using this straw tissue in the same way as gilding would be used in permanent decorations, as a ground on which to paint outlines in black or other dark colour.

Imitation coral letters can be made in the way described under the head of rice devices, on page 30.

Letters formed of everlasting flowers can be made so as to produce a good effect, as the colours available give the decorator the opportunity of arranging them in a variety of ways.

One of the simplest, and at the same time most telling Texts is made by simply painting in water colour (upon continuous cartridge paper) the whole lettering in black, dividing the words with finely traced ornament in red, and treating the capitals, of which there should be as few as possible, in the same manner. See Pls. XVI., XVII., and XIX.

The reason for using few capitals is this: each letter that rises above the others breaks the continuity of the "legend," and without due cause obtrudes itself upon the eye. In *Latin* inscriptions not even the name of God was written with a capital. In *English* we could hardly be content to use a small g.

If the initial and other capital letters are painted in red or blue, the body of the inscription should still be in *one colour*. Nothing is more destructive of "repose" than to see a text which tries to exhaust the paint box by its variety of hues; unless, indeed, the symbolism of colours is held as *de fide*.

Figs. 1 and 2, Pl. XVII., show the type of letter to be used for "cut out" texts in cardboard or other material. Fig. 3 shows the way in which to enlarge the letters to twice the size. By the same method, of course, they can be made 3, 4, or 6 or 8 times larger if it is needed. Four alphabets of small letters and three of capitals are given on Pls. XVI., XVII., and XVIII., for "hand painting."

These directions do not pretend to exhaust the whole subject of "Textual Decoration," but are simply intended to serve as hints; the reader's ingenuity will enlarge upon them, and it is to be hoped in so doing—improve. Many amateurs are to be found to whom they are wholly superfluous.

There is one caution to be given, however, in the matter of curved texts or legends, such as are placed over arches, frequently with the result of setting on edge the teeth of those who see them. It is of *absolute necessity* that a text round an arch should *follow its lines*. When making (or ordering) such a text,

 it is simply useless to expect that it will "fit," unless the radius of the curve is discovered. Some people imagine that to measure the length of the curve from A to A gives a sufficient measurement: a moment's thought will dispel this illusion. It is necessary to discover the "centres," of an arch, *i.e.*, the points from which the curves are struck.

Fig. 1104, Pl. XX., will perhaps render this more clear. Supposing that a text is required to fit close on to the outside moulding, or "label," or else to

come up to the edge of the splay, if there be no label moulding, or wherever it is required to come, let that be the curved line from т to υ (on either side). It is required to find the points *а and *в (*i.e.*, the radius from *а — w). If the arch is not too wide, stretch a lath or thin board across from т to т (being sure that the arch *does* begin to curve *there* †), then, by a few trials and shifting the bradawl backwards and forwards you will discover *а and *в. It is then necessary to measure the distance *between* these two points, or between s and either of them.

Then put down the measures, *а to *в, or *а to т, and т to т; and, if the arch is truly built, no more is needed. For the sake of corroborative evidence, however, it will be as well to measure from s to υ, and from υ to т.

These being true, the text will fit; otherwise, it is hopeless.

For other arches, " segmental " or four centred, a carpenter had better

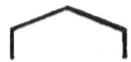 

be called in to strike the centres, as they are not so easily discovered by the amateur.

Another plan, which indeed is the only one practicable with large arches, is to fix nails at т т and υ. Having done this, stretch a string round the points of the triangle thus formed; then measure т to т, т to υ (on both sides), and from υ drop a line down to the centre of the string т—т and measure that; then measure from w to x on the *centre* of the curve, and from these measures the arch can be drawn out on a floor with sufficient accuracy.

A List of Texts is here given, which may be of use in suggesting " Words in Season."

FOR ADVENT.

" He cometh to judge the earth."
" Prepare ye the way of the Lord."
" Behold, thy King cometh unto thee."
" Be ye also ready. The Son of man cometh."
" The Son of man shall come in His glory."
" O come, O come, Emmanuel."
" Leva Jerusalem, oculos tuos."
" Veni Domine visitare nos in pace."
" Tu es qui venturus es."
" The night is far spent, the day is at hand."
" The Lord is at hand."

" The day of the Lord so cometh as a thief in the night."
" The day of Christ is at hand."
" Behold, He cometh with clouds; and every eye shall see Him."
" Surely I come quickly; even so, come, Lord Jesus."
" He shall come again in His glorious majesty to judge both the quick and the dead."
" Behold a virgin shall bear a son."

---

† Sometimes the spring of an arch is somewhat *above* the line of the capitals.

FOR CHRISTMASTIDE.

"There shall come a Star out of Jacob, and a Sceptre shall rise out of Israel."

"The right hand of the Lord bringeth mighty things to pass."

"The people that walked in darkness have seen a great light."

"Unto us a Child is born, unto us a Son is given."

"His name shall be called Wonderful, Counsellor, the Mighty God, the Everlasting Father, the Prince of Peace."

"There shall come forth a Rod out of the stem of Jesse, and a Branch shall grow out of his roots."

"The Lord, Our Righteousness."

"The Desire of all nations shall come."

"Behold, thy King cometh."

"The Sun of Righteousness shall arise with healing in His wings."

"Thou shalt call His name JESUS."

"Emmanuel! God with us."

"Hosanna to the Son of David."

"Hosanna in the highest!"

"The day-spring from on high hath visited us."

"Behold, I bring you glad tidings of great joy."

"Unto you is born this day a Saviour, which is Christ the Lord."

"Glory to God in the highest, on earth peace, good will toward men."

"Gloria in excelsis Deo et in terra pax hominibus bonæ voluntatis."

"Videbitis regem regum procedentem a procedentem a Patre tanquam sponsum de thalamo suo."

"Venite adoremus."

"Hodie nobis de coelo pax vera descendit."

"Verbum caro factum est."

"The Consolation of Israel."

"A Light to lighten the Gentiles."

"The Word was made flesh and dwelt among us."

"God sent forth His Son."

"God manifest in the Flesh."

"The Author of Salvation."

"The Finisher of Faith."

"We love Him because He first loved us."

"Now is come Salvation and Strength."

"King of kings and Lord of lords."

"The root and offspring of David, and the bright and Morning Star.

"God of God, Light of Light, Very God of Very God."

"God and Man: one Christ."

"Thou art the everlasting Son of the Father."

"Thou art the King of Glory, O Christ."

(The Circumcision.)

"His name was called Jesus."

"Circumcision is that of the heart."

"Oleum effusum nomen tuum."

FOR EPIPHANY.

"The people that walked in darkness have seen a great light."

"He shall bring forth judgment to the Gentiles."

"The Lord shall be thine everlasting life."

"The Gentiles shall see Thy righteousness."

"The Gentiles shall come unto Thee from the ends of the earth."

"Venit lumen tuum Jerusalem."

"Omnes venient aurum et thus deferentes. Alleluia."

"We have seen His star in the East, and are come to worship Him."

"When they saw the star they rejoiced."

"They presented unto Him gifts; gold, frankincense, and myrrh."

"A light to lighten the Gentiles."

Rejoice, ye Gentiles, with His people."

44

FOR LENT.

" The sacrifices of God are a broken spirit."
" God be merciful unto us."
" Have mercy upon us, O Lord."
" Fili dei miserere mei."
" Parce nobis Domine."
" De profundis clamavi."

" Let the wicked forsake his way."
" His mercy is on them that fear Him."
" Have mynde, have mercy."
" By thy fasting and temptation Good Lord deliver us."*

TEXTS FOR GOOD FRIDAY.

" He was despised and rejected of men."
" With His stripes we are healed."
" He was wounded for our transgressions."
" It is finished."
" He humbled Himself to the death of the Cross."
" Thou hast brought me into the dust of death."
" Deus meus respice in me."
" His own self bare our sins in His own body on the tree."

" By Thy Cross and Passion, good Lord, deliver us."
" By Thy precious death and burial, good Lord, deliver us."
" Behold, and see if there is any sorrow like unto my sorrow."
" Is it nothing to you all ye that pass by ? "
" O, my people, what have I done unto you."
" They crucified Him."
" They shall look on Him whom they have pierced.

FOR EASTER.

" I know that my Redeemer liveth."
" The Lord is King for ever and ever."
" He is risen."
" The Lord is risen indeed."
" I am the Resurrection and the Life."
" This Jesus hath God raised up."
" He whom God raised again saw no corruption."
" Christ was raised again for our justification."
" If we be dead with Christ, we believe that we shall also live with Him."
" Christ our Passover is sacrificed for us, therefore let us keep the feast."
" Now is Christ risen from the dead, the first-fruits of them that slept "
" As in Adam all die, even so in Christ shall all be made alive."

" O death, where is thy sting? O grave, where is thy victory."
" Death is swallowed up in victory."
" Our life is hid with Christ in God."
" I am He that liveth, and was dead; and, behold, I am alive for evermore."
" Lord of lords, King of kings."
" Alleluia! Alleluia! Alleluia!
" Alleluia! for the Lord God omnipotent reigneth."
" He is the very Paschal Lamb which was offered for us."
" Haec dies quam fecit Dominus: Exultemus et laetemur in ea. Alleluia."
" Resurrexit."
" Pascha nostrum."

* So for Lent and Passiontide any of the penitential verses of the Litany may be fitly used, either in Latin or English.

FOR ASCENSIONTIDE.

"Thou hast crowned him with glory and honour."

"The Lord sitteth King for ever."

"Thou, Lord, art Most High for evermore.

"He was received up into heaven, and sat on the right hand of God."

"Videntibus illis elevatus est."

"The Son of man, which is in heaven."

"He was taken up, and a cloud received Him out of their sight."

"He ever liveth to make intercession for them."

"Thou sittest at the right hand of God."

"He ascended into heaven."

TEXTS FOR WHITSUNTIDE.

"The Comforter, which is the Holy Ghost."

"They were all filled with the Holy Ghost."

"The Holy Ghost fell on all them that heard the word."

"The Spirit beareth witness, because the Spirit is Truth."

"Spiritus Domini replevit orbem terrarum."

"Spiritus qui a Patre procedit ille me clarificat."

"Thou only, O Christ, with the Holy Ghost, art most high in the glory of God the Father."

"The Holy Ghost came down at this time from heaven."

"The Holy Ghost, the Lord, and giver of Life."

"Veni Creator Spiritus."

FOR TRINITY SUNDAY.

"Holy, holy, holy, Lord God Almighty, which was, and is, and is to come."

"Not three Gods, but one God."

"Qualis Pater, talis Filius talis Spiritus Sanctus: Haec est Fides Catholica."

"Unitas in Trinitate, et Trinitas in Unitate veneranda."

"The Father is God, the Son is God, and the Holy Ghost is God."

"Glory be to the Father, and to the Son, and to the Holy Ghost."

"O holy, blessed, and glorious Trinity, three persons and one God."

"Gloria Patri et Filio et Spiritui Sancto: Sicut erat in principio et nunc et semper: et in saecula saeculorum."

TEXTS FOR HARVEST THANKSGIVING.

"While the earth remaineth, seed-time and harvest shall not cease."

"Man doth not live by bread alone, but by every word that proceedeth out of the mouth of the Lord."

"The earth is the Lord's, and the fulness thereof."

"Thou visitest the earth, and blessest it, Thou makest it very plenteous."

"Thou crownest the year with Thy goodness."

"Bless the Lord, O my soul, and forget not all His benefits."

"Wine that maketh glad the heart of man, and bread which strengtheneth man's heart."

"He maketh peace in thy borders, and filleth thee with the finest of wheat."

"Honour the Lord with thy firstfruits; so shall thy barns be filled with plenty."

"The harvest is the end of the world, and the reapers are the angels."

"The bread of life."

"In due season we shall reap if we faint not."

"O all ye green things upon the earth, bless ye the Lord."

FOR SCHOOL FEASTS.

" The fear of the Lord is the beginning of wisdom."

" Train up a child in the way he should go; and when he is old, he will not depart from it."

" Remember now thy Creator in the days of thy youth, while the evil days come not, nor the years draw nigh when thou shalt say, I have no pleasure in them."

" Suffer the little children to come unto Me, and forbid them not : for of such is the kingdom of God."

" Feed My lambs."

" Children, obey your parents in the Lord : for this is right."

" Keep innocency, and hold fast the thing which is right, for that shall bring a man peace at the last."

" Come ye children and hearken unto me : I will teach you the fear of the Lord."

Beside the texts here given there are scores, indeed hundreds, of others equally appropriate to the various seasons of the Church or special occasions. There are also many texts appropriate to the various parts of the Building. As for example—

THE PORCH.

" This is none other than the House of God, and this is the gate of Heaven."

" I will offer in His tabernacle sacrifices of joy."

" Enter into His gates with thanksgiving, and into His courts with praise."

" Peace be within Thy walls."

" I was glad when they said unto me, Let us go into the House of the Lord."

THE FONT.

" Suffer the little children to come unto Me, and forbid them not : for of such is the kingdom of God."

" In nomine Patris et Filii et spiritus sancti."

" Petite et accipietis."

" Spiritus ubi vult spirat."

" He that believeth and is baptized shall be saved."

" Repent and be baptized."

" One Lord, one Faith, one Baptism."

" Ye must be born again."

" Haurietis aquas in gaudio de fontibus salvatoris."

There is also the quaint Greek text, reading indifferently from left to right, or *vice versâ*—

ΝΙΨΟΝΑΝΟΜΗΜΑΜΗΜΟΝΑΝΟΨΙΝ,

Which the writer has seen quaintly Englished, thus—

" Wash off my sins from every part,
Not only face, but hands and heart."

It is evident that on any part of the Church there may be sacred words, which will emphasize the purpose for which it was designed. The following additional examples may suffice. On the chancel gate—

" Majestas domini per viam portae." *Ezek.* xliii. 4.

On the Retable (or elsewhere), this quaint device—

Q^{u} OS $_{Sa}^{A}$ NGUIS $_{M}^{D}$IRUS $_{Ch}^{T}$RISTI $_{M}^{D}$ULCEDINE $_{L}^{P}$AVIT
H

Or, " Deliciæ meœ cum filis hominum."

These and countless other texts, either from Holy Writ or the Services of the Church, may be written and read with profit.

When casting about for a suitable text for any given Festival, if one is not found in the foregoing list, read the Services for the Day in the Prayer Book, and either in Lessons, Psalms, Epistle, or Gospel some words are sure to occur " eloquent to the understanding."

It has not seemed needful to give the textual references " chapter and verse." A Cruden's concordance will supply the omission, should any text happen to be unknown to the reader.

CHAPTER IX.

SOME EMBLEMS OR SYMBOLS

USED IN DECORATION OF THE CHURCH.

It is manifestly impossible in a work of this size to give a complete list of all the emblems of Christ and his Saints, or of the countless symbols in which the faith of Christians has found expression. A few of the more common and better known are here set forth with such explanations as seem needful. Nearly all of them are figured on Plates X—XIV.

I.

THE HOLY NAME.

The two sacred names, official and personal of our Lord, as every one knows, are Χριστος Ἰησους.

How and why these two Greek names became represented and mis-represented in religious art by the various symbols employed from the days of the catacombs to these days of " decoration " is not so well known.

```
IHCOTC      In old " Uncial " MSS. the names read (1), and as
XPICTOC     contractions were frequently employed the same names
  (1)        are as likely as not to stand (2) written with three letters
IH    IHC   i.e., the first two and the last (of each word),    IC
XP    XPC   or with (3) simply the first and last letters, or   ――
(4)   (2)   (4) with the first two of each.                      XC
                                                                 (3)
```

The sign of Constantine the " Labarum " as it is called, is a monogram formed by the two first letters of the name Χριστος. Of this there are almost innumerable varieties, for example of which these may suffice.

In early times the name of *Christ* preponderated (naturally), since the name Jesus was not yet separated from common use and did not so clearly point to the Divinity.

Later on the tendency was in a direction exactly contrary, and *Jesus* prevailed.

**IhSYS
CRISTYS
bASILEW(N)
bASILEY
S**

It would appear that during the transitional period when the Greek names were becoming Latinized the seeds of error were sown.

The example here given (from an old coin) is a curious example of the process of crystallization, and it is the more remarkable that the same coin bears upon its reverse side the words

**EMMA NoYHΛ
ĪC   X̄C**

Here we have C = X, C = S, h = H, L = Λ, yet all seemingly interchangeable.

As the old Sigma (C) was much more like C than S it was accounted

I H C (5)
X P C

for emblematical purposes equivalent, and the two names appeared (5) in Roman lettering. Later on in Mediæval times they were written in black letter. But it is to be supposed that some person of

ihc (6)
xpc

moderate information was aware that the letter C really represented S; accordingly the monogram was written **i h s** (7).

The Renaissance found the **s** and preserved the letter while changing the type, giving us the familiar Jesuit monogram (8).

Tradition has not handed down the name of the ingenious derivator who *translated* this monogram into the words *Iesus Hominum Salvator*, which is about as reasonable (on antiquarian grounds) as the English rendering of a small child—I Have Suffered.

(8)   To return, however, a few centuries, the **h** was evidently too much for them, and, accordingly, the scribes who wrote the name of Jesus in full, left it there " stranded " between the other letters—**ihesus**. They knew that Jerusalem was written with H, and that S. Jerome had the same letter in his name, **hierusalem—hieronymus**, and, therefore, perhaps they felt it unfitting to write the greater name more scantily ! Accordingly, the name was

G

all but universally written *Ihesus*, not only in Latin, but also in English and French, until in Post-Reformation times, the h gradually dropped out as it had crept in.

When the sacred name is introduced into *mediæval* decoration, it should be spelt in the middle age fashion, **iḥesus, iḥc, iḥs,** or **xpc,** whereas in *Renaissance* work it should be written (in Roman letters) I.H.S. or X.P.C. Or if the symbols are preferred, thus :—

IHS. X.

II.

OTHER SYMBOLS OF OUR LORD.

AGNUS DEI.

Under this figure the Redeemer is constantly described in the Old Testament, as well as the New; and the Lamb was adopted in the earliest ages of Christianity as the type of our Lord, the most ancient perhaps being the figure of the lamb standing on a mount with the four rivers flowing from it. Some examples unite with the lamb the attributes of the Good Shepherd—viz., the crook and vessel of milk. Or the lamb is shown " as it were slain," either standing upon the altar, as in the famous picture of the adoration of the lamb, or lying upon the " book with the seven seals." The Agnus Dei is depicted with the peculiar nimbus of the Divinity, and carrying the cross, with the banner of the resurrection. Fig. 1, Pl. XI.

ALPHA AND OMEGA.

The first and last letters of the Greek alphabet are constantly used with the monogram of our Lord's name, with the cross, or as separate devices, Fig. 6c, Pl. XI.

ANCHOR.

The anchor is the emblem of hope, the cross-beam giving it a Christian signification as the emblem of faith. The heart, the emblem of charity, completes the symbols of the three graces. Fig. 12, Plate XI., etc.

THE CROSS—(See Plate XII).

" Among the first Christians, the instrument of God's suffering and " man's redemption, the Cross was made the chief emblem of their Faith, the " chief mark of their Community, their Standard and their Watchword." *

* Hope's Historical Essay on Architecture.

This " Sign of the Son of Man " on earth has taken many forms, nor is it easy to decide which was the shape of the " True Cross," since the σταυρος (or stake) used for crucifixion was not of necessity formed *crosswise*. Great difference of opinion has existed on this point.

Many have thought that the cross on which our Lord redeemed us was the " Tau," while others maintain that the Latin cross is the cross of Christ.

(*a*) *The Tau, or Egyptian Cross*, is, without doubt, pre-Christian, and may well have the name given to it by Didron, the " Anticipatory " Cross. Tradition gives this form to the wood carried by Isaac, and to the pole on which the brazen serpent was suspended.

The words of Ezekiel, ix, 4, " Transi in medio Jerusalem et signa Tau·super pontes virorum " are thus referred to by Tertullian—" Ipsa enim litera graecorum Tau nostra antem T species crucis." This type of cross, however, is usually given to the malefactors in representations of the crucifixion, partly, it may be presumed, because no " accusation " is shown.

The Labarum of Constantine is the T cross surmounted by a crown, containing the monogram of Christ, answering to the title which surmounted the actual cross of Christ, and which, according to the Roman custom, would be carried separately, declaring the name of the person to suffer and the cause of his punishment. To the horizontal bar of the Labarum was suspended a purple curtain resplendent with jewels. Our Lord is often represented in paintings of the resurrection carrying a Cross bannered in a similar manner.

(*b*) *The Latin Cross* is to us of the West naturally the most familiar form*, and either on this (or the Tau) our Lord doubtless hung. Hence it is called the Cross of the Passion.

(*c*) *The Greek Cross* differs from the Latin Cross, in having its four arms *equal*, instead of the lower being longer than the other three.

(*d*) *The Cross of Calvary* is the Latin Cross, mounted on three steps, figuring Faith, Hope, and Charity, which words are sometimes found inscribed on the steps, on "the *greatest* of which is Charity."

(*d*) *The Cross Fleurie* is, as the name implies, one with floreated ends. The Hymn, *Lustra sex*, aptly expresses the wish to show the tree changed from that of shame to that of glory.

> Crux fidelis, inter omnes
> Arbor una nobilis
> Nulla talem silva profert
> Fronde flore germine.

(*e*) *The Cross Fleurettée.*

---

* And, alas, by familiarity treated with contempt, being thought a fit adornment for watch chains and umbrellas !

(*f*) *The Maltese Cross* was borne by the Knight Templars, as also by the Knights of S. John.

(*g*) *The Patriarchal Cross* has a double cross bar.

(*h*) *The Papal Cross* has a triple one.

Other heraldic varieties used in " Blazonry " are—

(*i*) *The Saltire or Cross of St. Andrew (and St. Patrick).*

(*j*) *The Pointed Cross.*

(*k*) *The Cross Quadrate.*

(*l*) *The Cross Quarter*, pierced, or quarterly pierced (*l**).

(*m*) *The Cross Moline.*

(*n*) *The Cross Patonce.*

(*o*) *The Cross Pommée.*

(*p*) *The Cross Urdée.*

(*q*) *The Cross Crosslet.*

(*r*) *The Cross Fitchée* (*i.e.*, sharpened at the base).

(*s*) *The Cross Patée.*

(*t*) *The Cross Botonée* (or trefoiled).

(*u*) *The Cross Potent* (*u** the same rebated).

(*v*) *The Cross Fourchée.*

(*w*) *The Cross Recercelée.*

(*x*) *The Cross of Iona.*

Besides these there are others formed by the different heraldic " border " lines, *e.g.*, 7 and 3, are respectively engrailed and ragulée.

Any " charge " or device used in decoration may be represented cross-wise, or " in cross." Thus, four crowns, or crosses, or stars, or fleur-de-lys may be so arranged.

The smaller crosses, shown on Plates XII., and numbered 1—10, are examples of various oriental varieties, mostly of early date.

The Candle Stick (Fig. 7, Pl. XI.), with seven lights, is often found in early times. In later ages men preferred to " realize," and such a seven-branched light was in use on the altar of Durham Cathedral until compara-tively recent days.

The Hand.—Dextera domini (Fig. 31, Pl. XIV.), is not unfrequently found in ancient work. It is a suggestive emblem of Him who so often used His own hand to bless, and who now sitteth "at the right hand of the Father."

The Fish, which is indeed rather a "rebus" than an emblem, was very early employed to figure to us Him who made His disciples "Fishers of men;" but, secondarily, it was used to refer to Christians, who, like fish, *live by water*, as Tertullian says, "Nos pisciculi secundum ἰχθὺν nostrum in aquâ nascimur." The explanation of this anagram is sufficiently well-known Ἰησοῦς Χριστὸς Θεοῦ Υἱὸς Σωτήρ. Hence comes the symbolic use of the shape in Christian architecture, called the *vesica piscis*, (Fig. 11. Pl. XI.) the bladder of a fish having somewhat this form.

Three fishes interlaced are the common emblems of Baptism (Fig. 10, Pl. XI.)

The Lion is commonly (though possibly erroneously) taken as a symbol of Christ, the "Lion of the Tribe of Judah."

The Peacock is taken by Martigny and others as an emblem of the Resurrection. S. Augustine speaks of it as figuring immortality, and says that its flesh is incorruptible !

The Pelican (Fig. 2, Pl. XI.), shows us the love of Christ in leaving us the Sacrament, wherein "Our souls may be washed in His precious blood." The Pelican was supposed, in ancient times, to pierce her breast, either to feed her young or else to restore them when bitten by serpents.

The Phœnix (Fig. 3, Pl. XI.), though not of Christian origin, was readily adopted, in very early times, as a type of the Resurrection.

The Passion. Emblems of the suffering of Christ were very common in later mediæval times, either singly on shields or in groups. Carved or painted they are to be met with in bosses, screens, stall ends, windows; in fact, in almost every position.

The common emblems are the following :—

    (*a*)   The cross.

    (*b*)   The five wounds.

    (*c*)   The lantern, the swords and staves, the cock.

    (*d*)   The whips, rods and scourges, and the pillar.

    (*e*)   The spear, the reed, the basin and sponge.

    (*f*)   The crown of thorns.

    (*g*)   The vesture and dice.

    (*h*)   The three nails, the pincers and the hammer.

    (*i*)   The ladder.

    (*j*)   The label | I. N. R. I.

Most of these will be found figured on Plate X.

The Passion Flower was never represented in early art for the simple reason that it was unknown. On its first introduction to Europe it was supposed to be a " pious fraud " of the Jesuits, and its symbolism too complete to be true!

The only conventional representation (and one of the earliest, with which the writer is acquainted occurs in the " Tableau de la Croix" published in 1651. This, slightly altered, is drawn on Pl. XIII. (Fig. 14).

The Pomegranate (Fig. 23 and 24, Pl. XIV.) is taken either as a symbol of Christ's Royalty or of Immortality. It is shown either just *opening* and disclosing the wealth of *seed* within, or it is "voided" and filled with the monogram of our Lord, in 14th and 15th century embroidery; it is perhaps the commonest " flower."

The Rose and the Lily do not appear at first to have been used with any special reference to Christ—the Rose of Sharon and the Lily of the Valley; and when the brilliant scarlet hue of the said "lily" is taken into account the modern lily of the valley is scarcely its legitimate representative. The Rose was in later times, however, a favourite device; several are figured on Pl. XIV., Fig. 20 and 21, are *en soleil, i.e.*, with the glory of the sun.

The Star of Bethlehem, Fig. 13, Plate XI., is one of the commonest and best known of Christian emblems. Usually it has five points, sometimes seven (Fig. 14), and occasionally 9 (Fig. 8), when, however, it would more properly typify the nine-fold gifts of the Holy Spirit.

The Sun, Fig. 9, Plate XI., was often used in mediæval decoration, *probably* to typify our Lord—*Sol justitiæ*. Its use (with the moon) in representations of the Crucifixion is too well known to need more than mention.

The Ship or Ark (Fig. 5, Pl. IX.) is the emblem of the Church of Christ.

The Stag was a favourite emblem in mediæval times of the "desire " of Christians for the Sacraments.

The Blessed Sacrament. The emblem in mediæval times was the chalice with the circular bread (Fig. 5, Pl. X.), and perhaps no better or more scriptural one could be devised than "the cup which we bless, and the bread which we break."

The Good Shepherd. Under this guise our Blessed Lord was represented in the three first centuries, after which time the image died out, and has rarely, if ever, been reproduced until within the last few years.

The Vine is another ancient emblem of Christ (the True Vine), but it has never been much used since the fifth century; save in purely *decorative* form, as in running foliage in wood and stone carving, where it is far from probable that any reference was intended.

The common nineteenth century symbols of the sacrament, the "wheat and grapes," do not appear to have any sure foundation in antiquity.

The "*Whale*" of Jonah is another early emblem of Christ in his resurrection.

The Wise Men's Offering of Gold Incense and Myrrh, as also their three crowns, are Epiphany or Christmas symbols.

The Blessed Trinity.

The Triangle, or two interlaced Triangles, or again three Circles or a trefoil are sufficiently common emblems, but the most striking is the beautiful figure shown on Plate XI. (fig. 21); the octagon is the symbol of regeneration, the circle of eternity.

The Holy Spirit is shown by the Dove (Fig. 1, Pl. XIII.), or by the Flames of Pentecost ; so also by the seven foil, or by the seven lamps.

No representation of the Almighty Father was ever attempted in the purer days of Christian Art ; and although many late examples exist wherein the first person of the Blessed Trinity is shown with long beard and crowned with the Papal Tiara, it is enough to refer to such without attempting to reproduce them.

III.

EMBLEMS OF THE ANGELS.

THE ANGELS.

"The companion of S. Michael."

According to S. Dionysius and common tradition there are nine orders of angels, divided into three choirs.

I. COUNCILLORS. (Fig. 16, Pl. XIII.)

(*a*) *Seraphim.* Shown covered with eyes.

(*b*) *Cherubim.* With six wings, standing on *wheels*.

(*c*) *Thrones.* Shown with a throne or tower.

II. GOVERNORS. (Fig. 18.)

(*a*) *Dominations.* Shown with a sword, triple crown, sceptre, orb or cross.

(*b*) *Virtues.* Shown in full armour, with crown or censer.

(*c*) *Powers.* Shown holding a baton, or chaining devils.

III. MESSENGERS. (Fig. 17.)

(a) *Princedoms.* Holding a lily.

(b) *Archangels.*

>S. Michael trampling on the devil, or with a pair of scales.
>
>S. Raphael, with a pilgrim's staff, or fish and wallet.
>
>S. Gabriel, with a lily, or with sceptre and shield, bearing the name of the B.V.M.
>
>S. Uriel, a scroll and book.

(c) *Angels.* Shown bearing scrolls.

>Shields of the passion, musical instruments, etc. etc.

IV.

EMBLEMS OF THE EVANGELISTS AND APOSTLES.

(a) THE FOUR EVANGELISTS.

S. Matthew, the Angel. (Fig. 1, Pl. X.)

S. Mark, the Lion. (Fig. 2.)

S. Luke, the Ox. (Fig. 3.)

S. John, the Eagle. (Fig. 4.)

Sometimes these four are united in one, as described in the "Apocalypse" of Ezekiel, where the " Living creatures " had the " face of a man, an ox, a lion, and a flying eagle."

These same symbols have been applied also to the four archangels, the four doctors of the Western Church, and the four great prophets; but their use is now so generally confined to the Evangelists, that little uncertainty is likely to arise as to their meaning, if employed in Church decoration.

H

(b) THE EMBLEMS OF THE TWELVE APOSTLES

Will be found described under their names in § V.; one of each is represented on a shield on Plate XIII. (see Figs. 2—13). These emblems here
given are not the only ones; in fact, many of the twelve apostles counterchange
their emblems, and it is best to add the *names*, as in the examples figured.

V.

EMBLEMS OF THE SAINTS.

S. Agatha.	Breasts in a dish, an eye in pincers.
S. Agnes.	Lamb on a book, Lamb and palm.
S. Aidan.	A stag.
S. Alban.	Cross and square cap and sword.
S. Alphege.	A chasuble full of stones.
S. Ambrose.	A scourge, a beehive.
S. Andrew.	A cross saltire.
S. Ann.	The B. V. M. as a child by her side.
S. Anselm.	A vision of the B. V. M. and infant Saviour.
S. Anthony.	A crutched staff and bell, a pig with bell round its neck, a torch and bell, the devil in goat's form.
SS. Aquila and Priscilla.	Shoemaker's tools and tent.
S. Athanasius.	An open book, two columns.
S. Augustine of Hippo.	An inflamed heart, an arrow, an eagle, a child with spoon or shell by the sea shore.
S. Augustine of England.	Banner of the crucifixion, baptising King Ethelbert.
S. Barbara.	A tower and palm, or chalice.
S. Barnabas.	S. Matthew, gospel in the hand, three stones.
S. Bartholomew.	A flaying knife and a book.
S. Basil.	A lioness.

S. Benedict.	A cup on a book with serpent, a raven, a pitcher, a ball of fire.
S. Bernard.	The instruments of the passion, a white dog, a bee-hive.
S. Blaize.	Crozier and book, a wool comb, a pig's head.
S. Boniface.	Book pierced with sword, a scourge.
S. Bridget (of Kildare).	A flame over head.
S. Catharine.	A wheel set with spikes, hailstones descending on her torturers.
S. Cecilia.	An organ, a violin, a harp, a wreath of red roses.
S. Chrysostom.	A beehive, chalice on Gospels.
S. Christopher.	The Holy Child borne on the giant's shoulder, a lantern.
S. Clement.	Mitre, double or triple cross, anchor, a fountain.
S. Columba of Iona.	A bear's den.
S. Crispin.	Shoemaker's tools.
S. Cuthbert.	The head of S. Oswald, swans, and otters.
S. Cyprian	Gridiron and sword, books of magic burning.
S. Cyril.	The B. V. M. appearing.
S. David.	A dove on the shoulder.
S. Denis or Dionysius.	Mitred head carried in the hands or on a book.
S. Dominic.	A lily, a star on his forehead.
S. Dorothy.	Basket of fruit (and flowers).
S. Dunstan.	The Devil caught by pincers, a troop of angels.
S. Ethelburga.	The instruments of the Passion.
S. Edmund, King.	Arrows piercing him, arrow and sceptre.
S. Edmund, Bishop.	The Holy Child.
S. Edward, King & Martyr.	Dagger and cup, dagger and sceptre.
S. Edward, Confessor.	A sceptre, a ring held in left hand, a purse hanging from right arm. S. John's Gospel.
S. Elizabeth.	Shown saluting the B. V. M.
S. Elizabeth of Hungary.	A triple crown, a basket of bread, and flagon of wine.
S. Erasmus.	A windlass (with entrails wound round it).
S. Etheldreda.	A crozier and crown of flowers.

S. Enurchus.	A dove on the head.
S. Fabian.	A block at which he kneels, a dove, etc.
S. Faith.	An iron bed, book, and bundle of rods.
S. Francis of Assisi.	A crown of thorns, the stigmata.
S. Genevieve.	A shepherdess spinning.
S. George.	A dragon slain by him with spear.
S. Giles.	A hind, an arrow.
S. Gregory, Thaumaturgus	Devils driven out of a temple.
S. Gregory, Nazianzen.	Shown reading, Wisdom and Chastity appearing to him.
S. Gregory the Great.	Double barred cross, triple cross and tiara, A vision of Christ in his passion on the altar.
S. Helena.	The "True Cross," Church of Jerusalem in her hand.
S. Hilary of Poictiers.	An island with serpents, a child in a cradle.
S. Hubert.	A stag (on a book), a crucifix between its horns.
S. Hugh.	A vision of seven stars, a lantern, a swan.
S. Ignatius	In chains exposed to lions.
S. James the Great.	A pilgrim's staff, shell, hat and wallet.
S. James the Less.	A fuller's club, a saw.
S. Januarius.	A heated oven, a vial of blood.
S. Jerome.	A cardinal's hat, a lion.
S. Joanna.	An ointment box.
S. John, Baptist.	A lamb on book, a garment of camel's hair, a locust, a head on a dish.
S. John, Evangelist.	A cup with serpent coming out, an eagle.
S. Joseph.	A rod blossoming with lilies, a carpenter's square (or tools).
S. Jude.	A boat, a club, an inverted cross, a halbert.
S. Laurence.	A gridiron, a bag of money.
S. Leo.	On horseback, attila and soldiers kneeling.
S. Leonard.	An ox, chains and crozier.
S. Lucy.	Eyes in a dish (or on a book), a sword through her neck.
S. Luke.	An ox, a painting of the B. V. M.

S. Margaret.	A dragon chained.
S. Margaret of Scotland.	Shown visiting the sick, holding a black cross.
S. Mark	A lion, a fig tree.
S. Martin.	A goose, a beggar receiving half the Saint's cloak.
The Blessed Virgin Mary.	The lily, the marigold, the crowned M. R., the Fleur-de-Lys, the Ark of the Covenant, the serpent's head beneath her feet, &c.
S. Mary Magdalene.	A box of ointment, a skull.
S. Matthias.	A halbert or lance, a stone, a sword held by the point.
S. Matthew.	An angel, a dolphin, a money bag, a battle axe, a square, &c.
S. Monica.	A handkerchief and open book.
S. Nicholas.	Three children (in tub), three golden balls, an anchor.
S. Oswald King.	Sceptre and cross.
S. Pancras.	A sword and stone.
S. Patrick.	Serpents at his feet, a fire before him, the "trefoil" or shamrock.
S. Paul.	A sword (and book), three springs of water.
S. Perpetua.	A wild cow.
S. Peter.	A key, or two keys, one gold and one silver, a cock crowing, an inverted cross.
S. Philip.	A basket, two loaves and a cross, a spear and double cross.
S. Polycarp.	A pile of wood in flames.
S. Prisca.	A lion (or two lions), an eagle, a sword.
S. Remigius.	Carrying holy oils.
S. Richard.	A plough.
S. Rupert.	A salt box.
S. Sebastian.	A bunch of arrows, the same piercing him.
S. Simon.	A fish (or two fishes), an oar, a fuller's bat, a saw.
S. Stephen.	Stones in a napkin, in Dalmatic or in hand, or one on the head.
S. Sylvester	Constantine being baptised, an ox, a double cross, a tiara.

S. Thomas, Apostle.	A spear or lance, a square shown also touching the sacred wounds.
S. Thomas à Becket.	Pallium, archi-episcopal cross, sword across the back of his head.
S. Thomas Aquinas.	A star or sun on the breast, chalice and host.
S. Ursula.	An arrow, a dove, a book.
S. Vedast.	A wolf with a goose in its mouth.
S. Veronica.	The handkerchief with the Saviour's face.
S. Vincent.	An iron hook, a gridiron, a crow.
S. William of Norwich.	A crucified child, three nails.
S. William of York.	An Archi-episcopal cross.
S. Winifred.	A head carried in her hands.

A List of certain flowers appropriated to the various days in the calendar is here given, extracted from a book by W. A. BARRETT, *entitled,* "Flowers and Festivals."

JANUARY.

1. The Circumcision. Laurustinus, *Viburnum tinus.*
6. The Epiphany. Common Star of Bethlehem, *Ornithogalum.*
8. S. Lucian, P. M. Common laurel, *Laurus.*
13. S. Hilary, B. C. D. Barren strawberry. *Fragaria sterilis.*
18. S. Prisca, V. M. Four-toothed moss, *Bryum pellucidum.*
20. S. Fabian, B. M. Large dead nettle, *Lamium garganicum.*
21. S. Agnes, V. M. Black hellebore or Christmas rose, *Helleborus niger, Flore albo.*
22. S. Vincent, D. M. Early willow grass, *Draba verna.*
25. Conversion of S. Paul. Winter hellebore, *Helleborus hyemalis.*

FEBRUARY.

2. Purification B. V. M. Snowdrops, *Galanthus nivalis,*
3. S. Blasius, B. M. Great water moss, *Fontinalis antepyretica.*
5. S. Agatha, V. M. Common primrose, *Primula vulgaris.*
14. S. Valentine, B. M. Yellow crocus, *Crocus maesiacus.*

24. S. Matthias. Mezereon, *Daphne mezereum.*

MARCH.

1. S. David, Abp. C. Leek, *Allium porrum.*
2. S. Chad, B. C. Dwarf cerastium, *Cerastium pennilum.*
7. S. Perpetua, M. Early daffodil, *Narcissus pseudo, Narcissus simplex.*
12. S. Gregory, B. C. D. Channelled ixia, *Ixia bulbocodium.*
17. S. Patrick, B. C. Shamrock, trefoil, *trifolium repens.*
18. S. Edward, K. M. Great leopard bane, *Donoricum pardalionetes.*
21. S. Benedict, Abb. Herb bennet, *Genon urbanum;* and way bennet or wild rye, *Hordeum murinum;* also, bulbous fumitory, *Fumaria bulbosa.*
25. The Annunciation. Marigold, *Calendula officinalis.*

APRIL.

3. S. Richard, B. C. Evergreen alkanet, *Anchusa sempervirens.*
4. S. Ambrose, B. C. D. Meadow orchis, *Orchis mascula.*
19. S. Alphege, Abp. M. Ursine garlic, *Ilium Aursinum.*
23. S. George, M. Harebell, *Hyacinthus nonscriptus.*
25. S. Mark. Clarimond tulip, *Tulipa praecox.*

MAY.

1. S. Philip. Red tulip, *Tulipa Gesneri*.
3. Invention of the Cross. Poetic narcisse, *Narcissus poeticus*.
19. S. Dunstan, Abp. C. Monkshood, *Aconitum Napellus*.
26. S. Augustine, Abp. C. Rhododendron, *Rhododendron ponticum*.
27. Ven. Bede, P. C. Yellow bachelor's button, *Ranunculus acris plenus*.

JUNE.

1. S. Nicomede, P. M. Single yellow rose, *Rosa lutea*.
5. S. Boniface, B. M. Three-leaved rose, *Rosa sinica*.
11. S. Barnabas. Midsummer daisy, *Chrysanthemum leucanthemum*.
17. S. Alban, M. Feather grass, *Stipa pennata*.
24. Nativity of S. John Baptist. S. John's wort, *Hypericum pulchrum*. Tutsam, *Hypericum Androsæmum*. Chrysanthemum, also gooseberries.
29. S. Peter. Yellow rattle, *Rhinanthus Galli*.

JULY.

2. Visitation B. V. M. White lily, *Lilium candidum*.
15. S. Swithun, B. C. Small cape marigold, *Calendula pluvialis*.
20. S. Margaret, V. M. Virginia dragon's-head, *Dracocephalus virginianum*.
22. S. Mary Magdalene. African lily, *Agapanthus umbellatus*.
25. S. James. S. James' cross, *Amaryllis formosissima*. S. James' wort, *Senecio Jacobæa*.
26. S. Anne. Common chamomile, *Matricarica chamomilla*.

AUGUST.

Lammas Day, *i.e.* "S. Peter ad Vincula." Stranomy, *Datura stramonium*.
6. Transfiguration. Common meadow saffron, *Colchicum autumnale*.
7. Holy Name of Jesus. Common amaranth, *Amaranthus hypochondriacus*.
10. S. Lawrence, D. M. Common balsam, *Impatiens balsama*.
15. Assumption B. V. M. Virgin's bower, *Clematis vitalba*.
24. S. Bartholomew. Sunflower, *Helianthus annuus*.

28. S. Augustine, B. C. D. Golden rod, *Solidago virgurca*.
29. Beheading of S. John Baptist. S. John's wort, *Hypericum elodes*.

SEPTEMBER.

1. S. Giles, Abb. S. Giles' orpine, *Sedum telephium*.
7. S. Enurchus, B. C. Starwort, *Callitriche autumnalis*.
8. Nativity, B. V. M. Bryony, our Lady's Seal. Red berried bryony, *Bryonia dioica*.
14. Holy Cross day. Blue passion flower, *Passiflora cærulea*.
17 S. Lambert, B. M. Narrow-leaved mallow, *Malva angustifolia*.
21. S. Matthew. Cilcated passion flower, *Passiflora cilcata*.
26. S. Cyprian, Abp. M. Starwort, *Aster tripolium*.
29. S. Michael and All Angels. Michaelmas daisy. *Aster tradescanti*.
30. S. Jerome, P. C. D. Golden amaryllis, *Amaryllis aurea*.

OCTOBER.

1. S. Remigius, Abp. C. Lowly amaryllis or S. Remy's lily, *Amaryllis humilis*.
6. S. Faith, V. M. Late feverfew, *Pyrethrum scrotinum*.
9. S. Denys', B. M. Milky Agaric, *Agaricus factiflorus*.
17. S. Etheldreda, Q. V. C. Ten-leaved sunflower, *Helianthus decapetalus*.
18. S. Luke. Floccose agaric, *Agaricus floccosus*.
25. S. Crispin, M. Flea-bane starwort, *Aster conizoides*.
28. SS. Simon and Jude. S. Simon, late chrysanthemum, *Chrysanthemum scrotinum*. S. Jude, scattered starwort, *Aster passiflorus*.

NOVEMBER.

1. All Saints. Sweet bay, *Laurus nobilis*. Dark red sunflower, *Helianthus atro rubens*.
6. S. Leonard, D. C. Yew, *Taxus baccata*.
11. S. Martin, B. C. Weymouth pine, *Pinus strobus*.
13. S. Britius or Brice, B. C. Bay, *Laurus boeticus*.

15. S. Machutus, B. C.   Sweet colesfoot, *Tussilago fragrans.*

17. S. Hugh, B. C.   Free stramony, *Datura arborea.*

20. S. Edmund, K. M.   Red stapelia, *Stapelia rufa.*

22. S. Cecilia, V. M.   Trumpet-flowered wood sorrel, *Orchis tubiflora.*

23. S. Clement, B. M.   Convex wood sorrel, *Oxalis convexula.*

25. S. Catherine, V. M.   Sweet butter bur, *Petasites vulgaris.*

30. S. Andrew.   S. Andrew's cross, or common ascyrum, *Ascyrus vulgaris.*

DECEMBER.

6. S. Nicholas, B. C.   Nest-flowered heath, *Erica nidiflora.*

8. Conception B. V. M.   Abor vitæ, *Thuja occidentalis.*

13. S. Lucy, V. M.   Cypress abor vitæ, *Thuja cupressoides.*

21. S. Thomas.   Sparrow wort, *Erica passerina.*

25. Christmas.   Holly, *Ilex bacciflora.*

26. S. Stephen, Proto-M.   Purple heath, *Erica purpurea.*

27. S. John.   Flame heath, *Erica flamma.*

28. Holy Innocents or Childermas.   Bloody heath, *Erica cruenta.*

31. S. Sylvester, B. C.   Genista heath, *Erica genistopha.*

MOVABLE FEASTS.

Passion Sunday.   Christ's thorn, *Palisus aculeatus.*

Palm Sunday.   Common palma Christi, *Ricinus communis.*

Maundy Thursday.   Laurel-leaved passion flower, *Passiflora rubra.*

Good Friday.   Long-sheathed anemone, *Anemone pulsatilla;* also called passion flower.

Easter Eve.   Spear-leaved violet, *Viola lactea.*

Easter Day.   White lily, *Lilium candidum.*

Rogation Sunday.   Rogation flower, *Polygala vulgaris.*   Common milkwort.

Ascension Day.   Lilies of the valley, *Convallaria majalis.*

Whitsun Day.   Columbine, *Aquilegia vulgaris.*   White thorn, *Prunus spinosa.*

Trinity Sunday.   Herb Trinity, *Viola tricolor;* also called Pansy, Violet, Heart's-ease. Common white trefoil, *Trifolium repens.*

VI.

SHIELDS

Are the commonest vehicles for emblems.   Whether from a sense of being suitable for the use of the Church "Militant," or, from the encroachments of Heraldry on Church decoration, is uncertain.   The Shield is capable of an infinite variety of shaping, from the early three-cornered form to the grotesque escutcheons, which used to glare upon our childish eyes from the hatchments suspended on Church walls, whenever "a great man was dead."

On Plate XIII. the Emblems of the Twelve Apostles are, for convenience, charged on Shields of various designs, arranged, more or less, chronologically, as regards their shape.   Fig. 1, on which the Sacred Dove is drawn, shows the typical early English Shield (which was for sometime, however, much *longer*). Figs. 2 and 4 show shapes a trifle later, while the rest in a descending scale, carry us to the 16th century; further than this it is not advisable to venture.

VII.

CROWNS.

So distressing are the common forms, that the writer has thought it worth while to make a somewhat extensive collection of examples, ranging from 1100 to 1500. Some of these are sketched from Parker's Glossary, some from Viollet le Duc, and some from other sources. They may all be depended on as " authentic," and it is hoped they will commend themselves to the decorator as decidedly preferable to the spiky articles too commonly in use.

VIII.

FLEUR-DE-LYS.

Of these, five examples are given on plate XIV., Figs. 25—29; it is probable, however, that the Parish Church in which the reader worships, will provide as good, or better examples.

IX.

COLOURS.

The writer must plead to a certain amount of scepticism in the matter of symbolism ; as applied to colour it is commonly said that each colour has its meaning, and that the mediaeval artists *never* used colour save with due regard to its significance—Credat Judæus ! However, there is some truth in the belief, and as regards the "liturgical" colours,* commonly used at the present time, there is little obscurity.

White signifies rejoicing, purity, and light ; hence it is used at Christmas and Eastertide, on Trinity Sunday, and on Feasts of the Blessed Virgin, etc.

Red shows Divine Love, fire and blood, hence its use on Whitsunday and on Martyrs' Feasts.

Purple or Violet is the colour of mourning and penitence, and, therefore, it is used in Advent from LXX. Sunday to Easter Eve, and on Ember Days and Vigils' Rogation Days, and on the Feast of the Holy Innocents (save on a *Sunday*, when red is used).

Green is the colour of repose, and is used in Trinity season and after Epiphany, for whatever " blank " time there is before LXX.

* No venture must be made on the thin ice of "sarum colouris," a subject tempting, no doubt, but too vast to be treated, save in a separate book.

I

Blue is the colour of the Blessed Virgin; it is also called the colour of heaven.

Gold, they say, signifies glory. Aptly enough; but why *grey* should figure "innocence falsely accused," the writer is at a loss to explain.

A few words must be added on the *heraldry* of colour, which is specially important when emblems are placed upon *shields*.

The heraldic " colours " are five—

Red (*gules*), blue *azure*), green (*vert*), black (*sable*), purple (*purpure*).

The " metals," two—

Gold (*or*), and silver (*argent*).

And with regard to their use, the rule to which attention must be drawn is this:—a *metal* must not be put upon a metal, nor a *colour* upon a colour. Hence if a shield is *blue* a *red* cross must not be put upon it; nor if it is *silver* (*i.e.*, *white*) must anything be charged on it in *gold*; but a red or blue, or green ground, must be charged with gold or silver, and a gold or silver ground with colour.

Care should be taken to avoid a meaningless, or *too meaning*, use of heraldic figures, " bars," " chevrons," etc.; and above all take care what is done with a bend  which, when reversed, is the mark of illegitimacy.

The writer once saw it hung up as an appropriate decoration opposite the tomb of a nobleman, whose first ancestor *had* that stain on his escutcheon

CHAPTER X.

STRUCTURAL DECORATION.

1.—ARCHES AND COLUMNS.

A few examples are given on Plate VI., showing the various treatments suggested. After all, however, it must be considered in each case how the object lends itself to ornamentation. Observation and experience are the only sure guides; and a few failures at first will lead to success sooner or later. The cautions in Chapter II. will, it is hoped, preserve the decorators from the many pit-falls into which their predecessors have been snared. The frontispiece of the book shows perhaps how far it is advisable to go in this direction.

Bear in mind that just as plain spaces and not ornament are to be covered, so in an arch or column it is always a *hollow or receding*, and not a *projecting* member, that invites foliage.

Sometimes it is safe, when the columns are *tall*, to form a dado about 3 feet 6 inches high, by sewing light serge or cotton tightly round the column, on the top of which a light cresting of leaves, or a decorated border may be tied.

2.—WALL SPACES.

Whatever words might be said on this matter have been fully anticipated in the earlier pages of the book, and the reader can refer to them.

3.—WINDOW SILLS

Can be very effectively decorated by procuring a board about an inch thick, cut to the shape of the sloping sill, and having it perforated with holes all over about two inches apart, and sticking sprigs of evergreens into these holes, covering the board with moss. Another plan is to fit boards into all the window sills, and cover them with moss or leaves, and form a text in everlasting flowers to run all round the Church.

Texts on the same plan can of course be formed in various ways, such as in straw tissue on a flock ground; or if it is preferred, a device, instead of a text, may be placed in the centre of each window sill on the groundwork of leaves or moss.

The texts can also be illuminated in colours on calico or cartridge paper, and surrounded with wreaths of evergreens. See Figs. 7, 8, 9, Pl. VI.

Here it is desirable to remark that wherever damp moss, or any other material likely to leave a stain on the stonework, is used, it will be requisite to put waterproof paper, or something of a like nature, underneath it. For this reason the French dried moss is generally preferable for decorative purposes, and it is also a better colour. For various suggestive sketches see Plate VII., Plate I., &c.

4.—SCREENS

Had better be left alone as much as possible. Metal is damaged more or less certainly by contact with damp leaves. Wooden screens are hard to decorate without the use of nails.

It is often feasible however, to lay a wreath of evergreens along the top beam, or to sketch a text across the whole length. Troughs filled with moss and flowers can be set at the foot of the panelling, and sometimes the panels themselves (if plain) may be thus decorated. See Pl. VIII., Fig. 1—4.

Cut out panels in cardboard exactly the size required, and ornament them with illumination, appliqué work, as may be preferred: to fix them in their places, " spring " in thin laths of wood in front of them, and they will be as firm as if they were nailed. Roses or other flowers in the zinc cones already mentioned may be hung at intervals, but little in the way of " wreathage " had better be attempted if the uprights and arches are well proportioned as they stand; they will not be improved by being *thickened* with leaves.

5.— PULPITS

Require special care, and so much depends on their form and design, that it is impossible to give any very definite hints for their decoration; narrow wreaths stitched on to canvas, or fixed to wire, may be perhaps safely put round the heavier mouldings. Flowers may be suspended, and the base surrounded with flowers in pots. See Fig. 13, Pl. IX.

6.—FONTS.

Great variety may be obtained by the use of different " covers " of wire-work, wreathed with foliage. If the font be plain, it is very easy to fasten bands round the bowl, and to decorate the base with growing flowers. If the font stand on steps, these may be well banked with moss (using waterproof paper), and decked with flowers; texts and devices being perhaps introduced formed of everlastings. Three examples are given of ancient Fonts. Figs. 11 and 12, Pl. IX., and Fig. 7, Pl. VIII.

7.—ALTARS

Should never be touched; if it be the custom in a Church to use Frontals of different colours then the covering will be sufficient decoration. Vases filled with flowers can be placed upon the ledge at the back, and ferns, flowers and small shrubs placed on either side, provided always that they do not, by blocking up the space, hinder the clergy in their ministrations. Pl. I. shows an altar with the fullest decoration advisable.

8.—Communion Rails, Stalls and Lecterns.

These, in the opinion at least of the writer, are best unadorned, for the reasons set forth in Chapter II. If any ornament is introduced it should be of the slightest possible description.

These directions read as very meagre ones it must be admitted, but so much depends on the character of the building that few rules of universal application are to be laid down. The writer in conclusion can only say :—

" Sit modus in rebus."

CHAPTER XI.

MATERIALS.

All particulars as to materials and ready-made decorations will be found in the Appendix. It may be advisable, however, in this place to set down a list, capable of considerable expansion, of such things as are likely to be required by the amateur church decorator. To begin with evergreens. Of the holly, which is by custom the principal one used, there are sixteen varieties, the common one being the *Ilex Aquifolium.*

Holly.	Fir (in its various varieties).	Privet.
Variegated Holly.	Arbor Vitæ.	Myrtle.
Ivy (the smaller variety).	Portugal Laurel.	Cypress.
Laurel.	Arbutus.	Bay.
Box.	Laurustinus.	Rosemary.
Yew.	Ferns.	Moss.

MATERIALS FOR FORMING WREATHS.

Evergreens, as previous list.	Reel wire (as used by artificial	Pliers (for wire).
Everlasting flowers.	flower-makers).	Hammer.
Imitation Holly berries.	Needles and thread.	Nails and tacks.
Rope.	Hoop iron.	Frame for decorated font cover.
Stout string.	Deal laths.	Bands of perforated zinc.
Fine twine.	Scissors (best tied by a long tape	Letters of do. do.
Stout iron or copper wire.	to wrist or waist when in use).	Zinc and iron clips for capitals
Fine do. do.	Pocket knife.	of columns.

FOR EVERGREEN OR FLOWER DEVICES.—-The groundwork cut out in perforated zinc in addition to the foregoing.

FOR WORKED AND PAINTED DEVICES.—Full-sized models of monograms, crosses and devices.—These are best procured cut out in cardboard, unless the amateur has sufficient knowledge of drawing to set them out himself.

Cloth (in various colours).	Gold paper.	Gold leaf.
Cotton-velvet do.	Silver paper.	Gold size.
Cotton-wool.	Straw tissue.	Paint brushes.
Cartoon paper.	Prepared (painted) cloth.	Straight rule.
Coloured papers.	Prepared calico.	Set square.
Coloured flock papers.	Paints, prepared for use.	Compasses.

For large circles, a nail or pin, driven in at the point from which the circle is struck, with a string of the required length (having a pencil attached), revolving round it, forms a good substitute for compasses.

Plate
i

an Altar decorated for Christmas

Plate
ii

Plate iii

1

2

Plate iv

Temporary Rood-screen:

Plate V

elo pax vera descendit ✠   Christus venit : lumen tuu

omnia opera domini domino : lauda

Temporary Screen and divers decorations:

Thos. Parton & Co. Photo Litho 443 Wandsworth Road London S.W

Plate vj

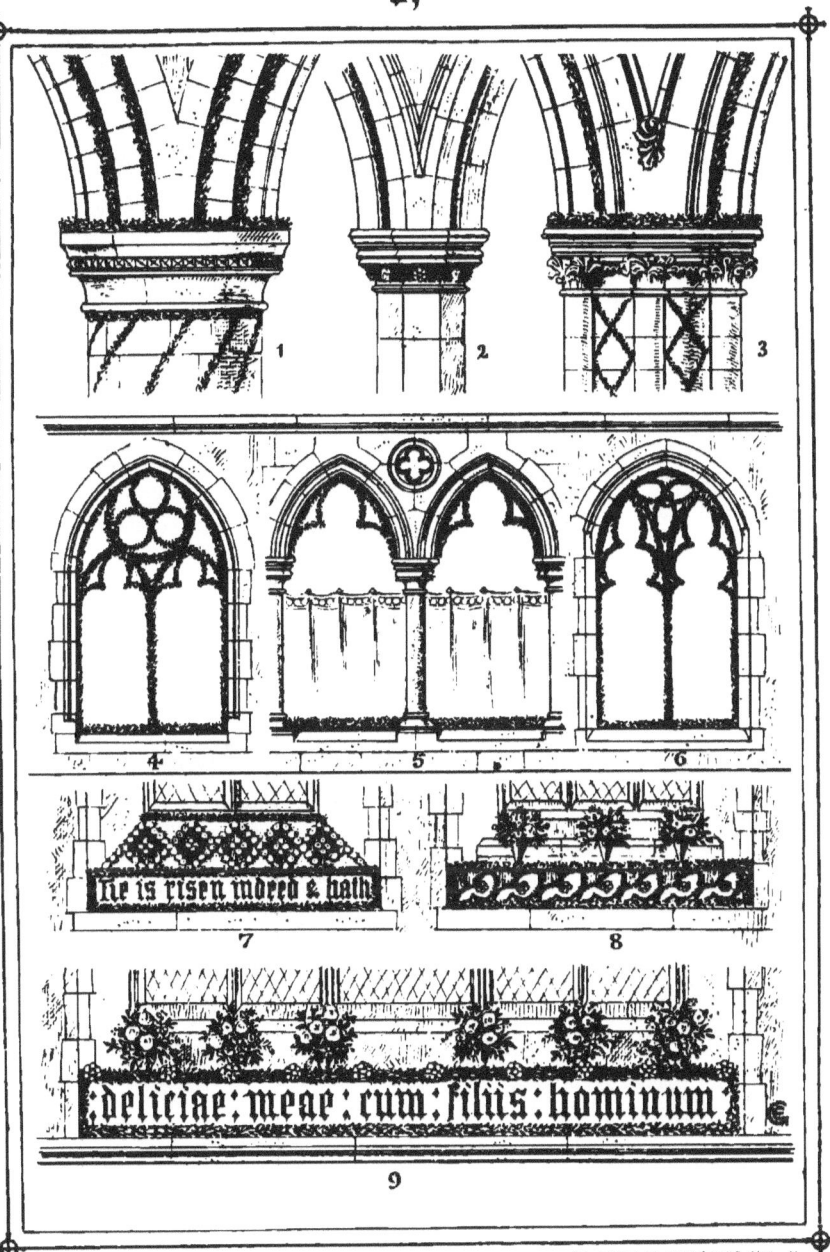

7. he is risen indeed & hath

9. deliciae : meae : cum : filiis : hominum

Plate
vij

Plate
viij

the Font in Croyland Abbey

Plate
IX

FONT in SEVINGTON (Kent.)

FONT in KIRKBY-MISPERTON

Plate
X

Emblems of the Passion:

Plate
xi

Plate
XII

Gammadia[2]

Anchor Cross
(Didron)

Anchor Cross
(Martigny)

j

k

a

d

b

n

m

5

6

y

v

c

p

z

7

8

t

e*

o

x

w

e

u*

r

q

g

h

u

T

9

10

f*

f

i

l

l*

s

s

Plate XIII

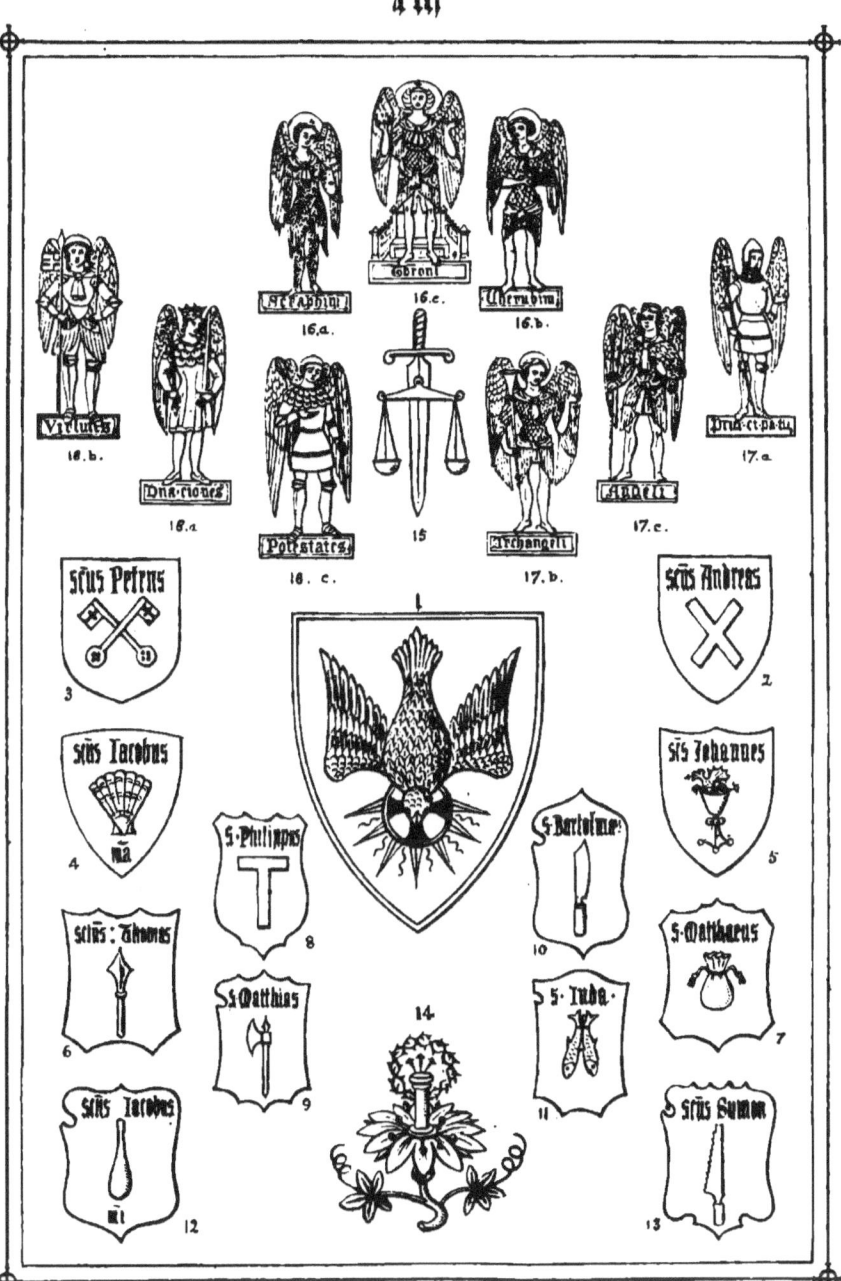

16.a. Sctaphini
16.c. Throni
16.b. Cherubim

Virtutes 16.b.
Dnacioues 18.a
Potestates 16. c.

15

Archangeli 17.b.
Angeli 17.c.
Prin-ci-pa-tu. 17.a

Scūs Petrus 3
Scūs Andreas 2

Scūs Iacobus mā 4
S. Philippus 8
S. Bartolmeº 10
Scūs Iohannes 5

scīus : Thomas 6
S. Matthias 9
S. Iuda. 11
S. Matthaeus 7

Scūs Iacobus mī 12
14
Scūs Simon 13

Plate
xiv

10

11

1200

1150 12

1200 13

18

1100 14

1250 2

1130 5

19

20

1300 3

4

21

Font, Prittlewell.

1400 5

31

from Ancient Baton

16

6

17

1450

24

23

1450 7

1485 8

22

30

Font, Prittlewell.

Font, Prittlewell.

25

26

9
1500

28

29

27

Plate XV

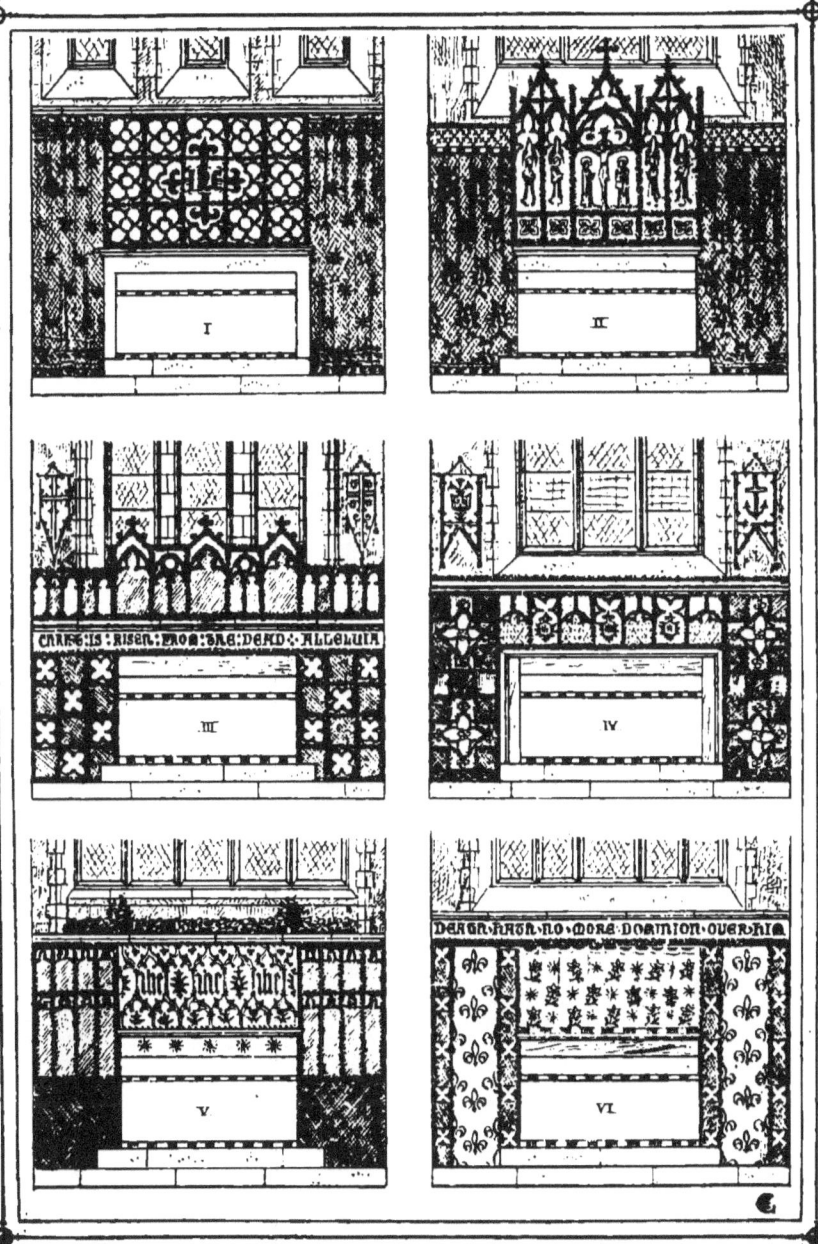

I

II

III

CHRIST IS RISEN FROM THE DEAD ALLELUIA

IV

V

VI

DEATH HATH NO MORE DOMINION OVER HIM

Plate
xvi

PQRSUW

XPZ abcdefgh

ijklmnopqrſstvvw

xyz

Plate
xviii

ABCDEFGHIJK

LMNOPQRSTUV

WXYZ abcdefghijkl

mnopqrstuvwxyz.✝

I·II·III·IV·V·VI·VII·VIII·IX·X

1

2

ABCDEFGHIJKLM

NOPQRSTUVWX

abcdefghijklmnopqrstuv

wxyz 123456789 YZ.

Chas. Forton & C° Photo Litho. 449. Wandsworth Road, London S.W.

Plate
xix

Plate
XX

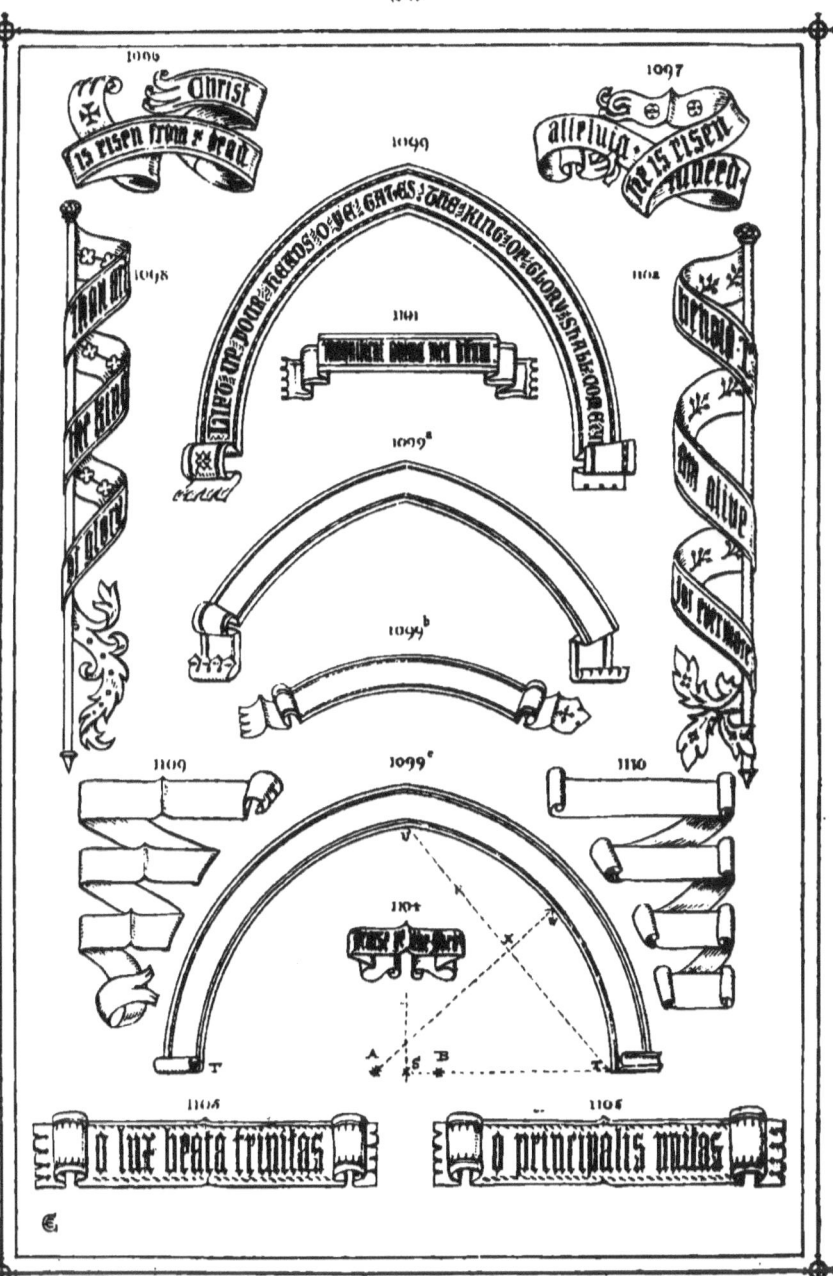

Plate
xxi

Plate
XXII

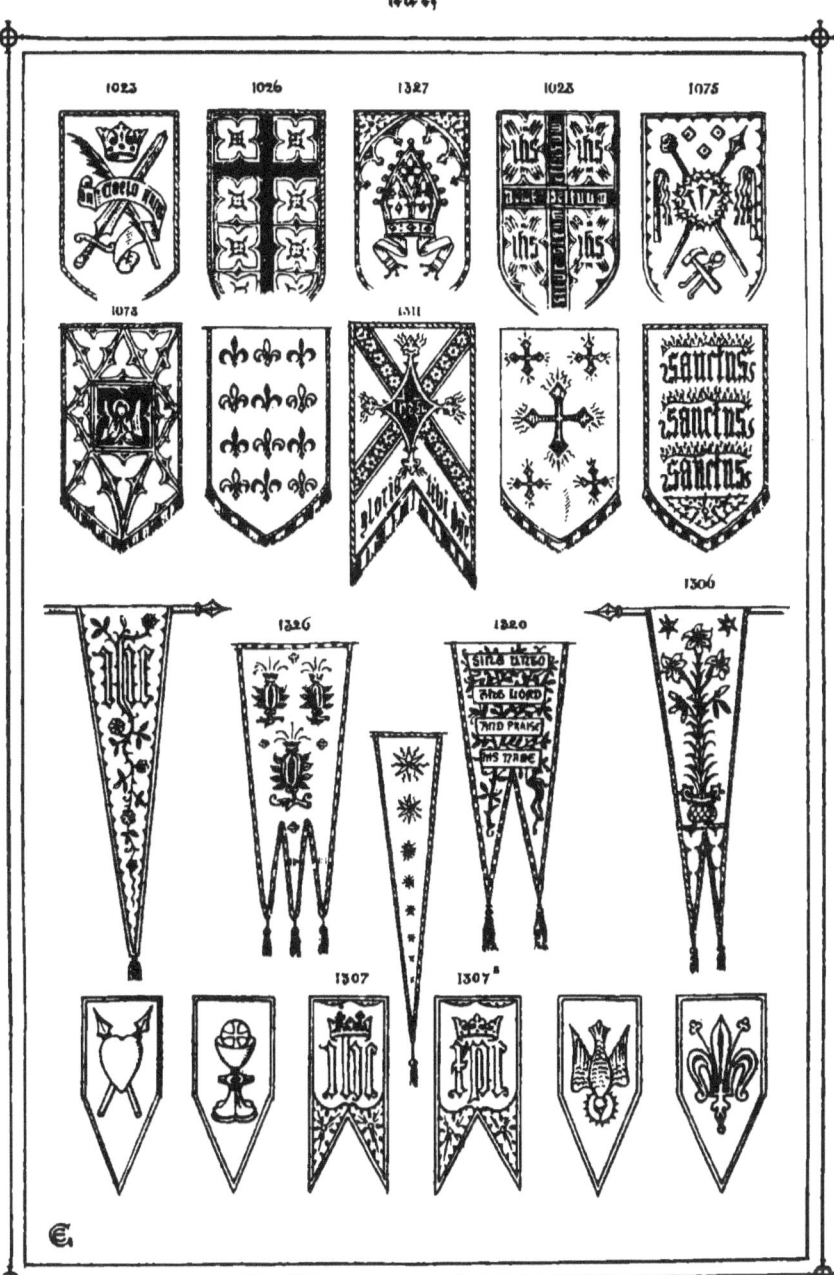

Plate
xxiii

Plate
XXIV

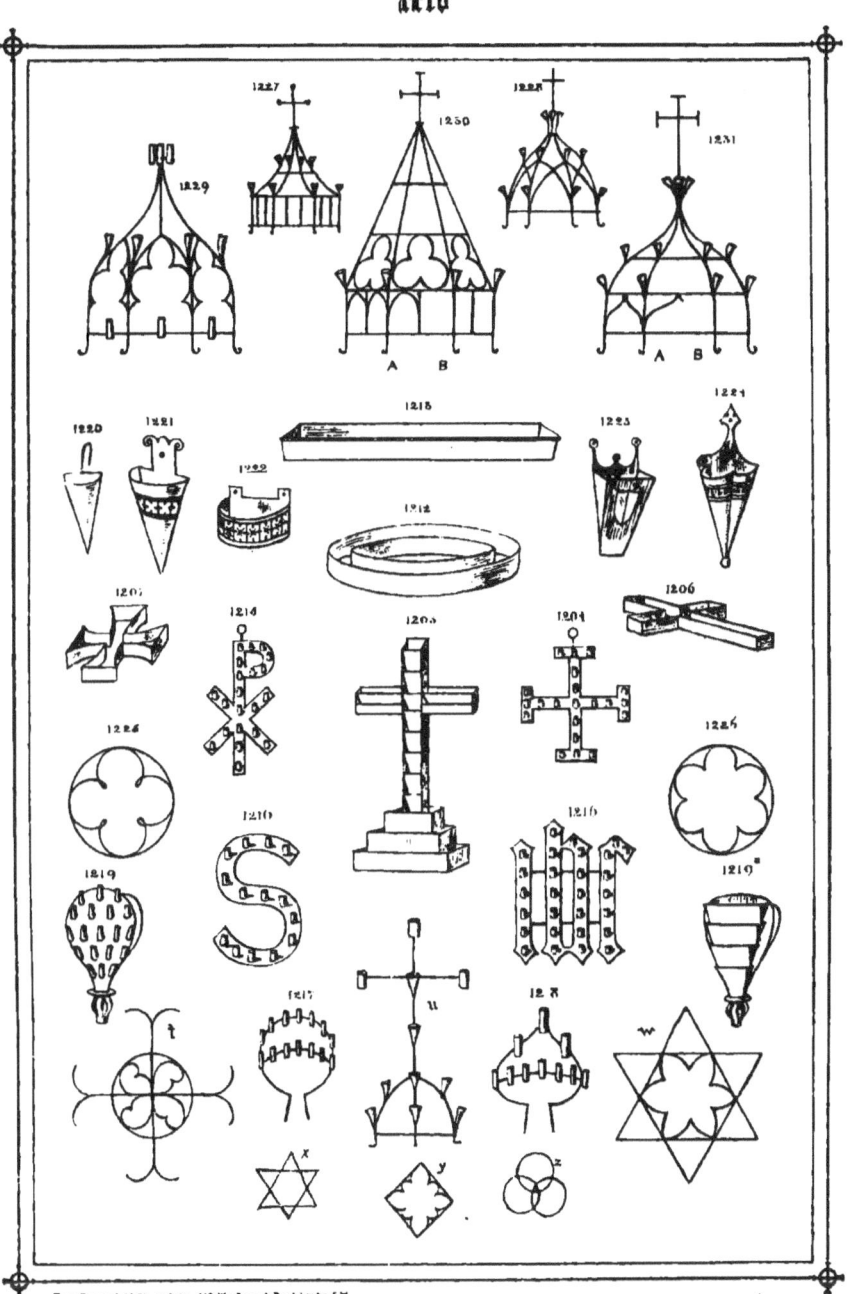

Plate
XXV

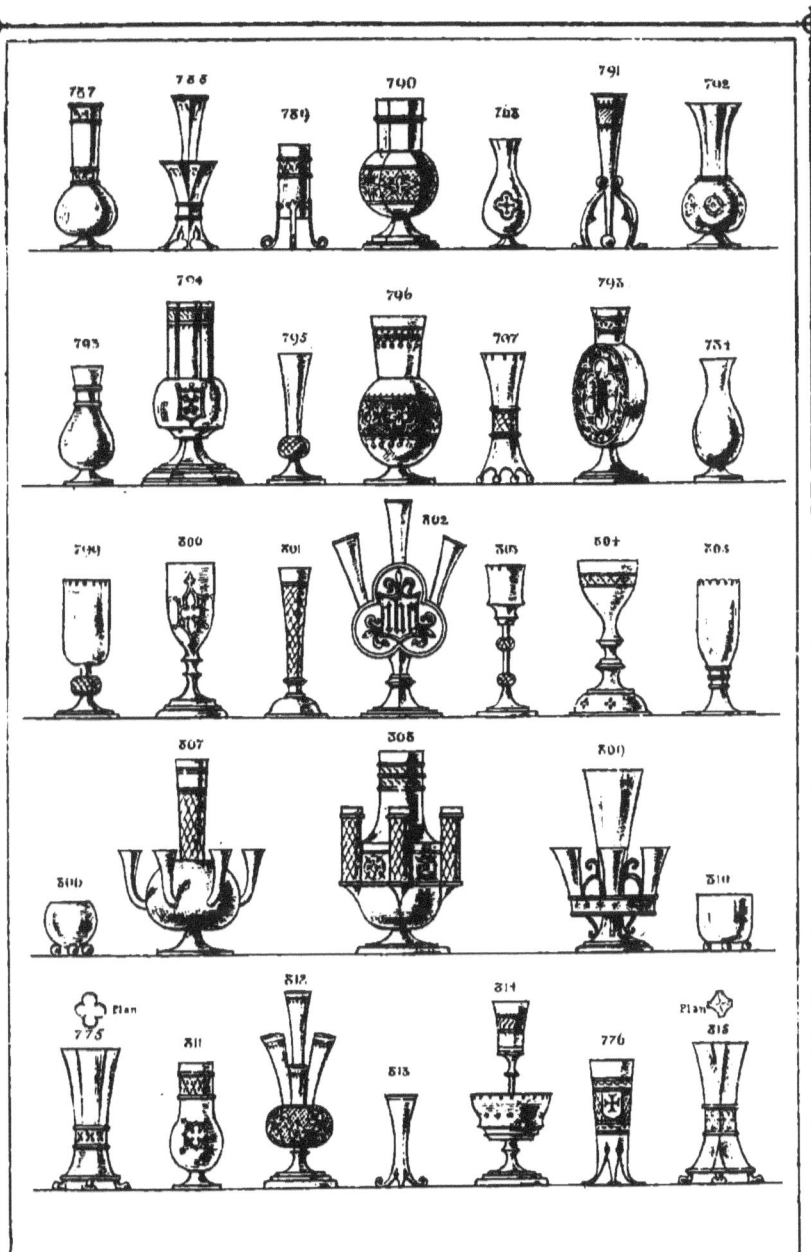

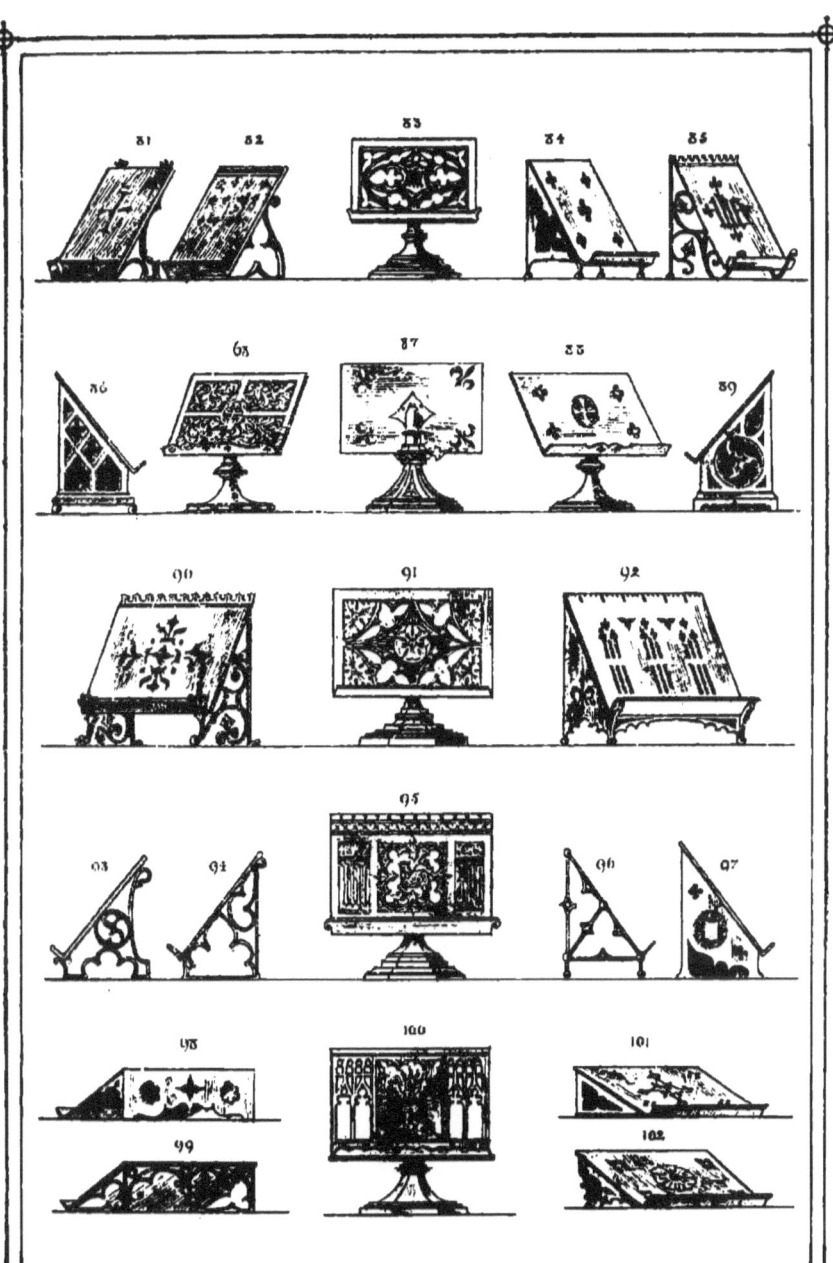

www.ingramcontent.com/pod-product-compliance
Lightning Source LLC
Chambersburg PA
CBHW020753020726
47495CB00008B/2413